The
End
is
Insight

The
End
Is
Insight

A Karmic
Life-Journey

by
Jim Fox

**Published by
The Centre of the Labyrinth**

First published and distributed in the United Kingdom by:

The Centre of the Labyrinth
The Centre, 1 Pell Street, Swansea, SA1 3ES
Tel.: (44) 1792 477123
www.thecentre-swansea.co.uk

A catalogue record for this book is available from the British Library

ISBN 978-0-9573855-5-9

**Dedicated,
with much gratitude,
to everyone who has
been there along
the way**

Contents

Don't waste your life for that which can be taken away . . .

Osho

Introduction

The following is my story.

Although not a full and comprehensive account, it is a picture of my journey from birth up until this present moment. In these pages I want to introduce you to the influences, decisions, people and places that, together, have helped to map out my journey.

Everything that happens in one's life is important, every choice, every response, every situation, every conversation, there is nothing that does not affect one's development. Where we are now is a result of all that has gone before, and all that has gone before has led us to where we are now.

I have no regrets, and I am grateful for all the things and all the people that I have encountered on my journey. My hope is, as you read these words, that you too will come to realise that everything in your life has been working together to sculpt you into what you now are, and also that every encounter that you have with another, is working with all the other influences to mould that other person's life.

Zen and The Lion

I once heard a very old Zen story; it was tale of a lion cub that had been adopted by a flock of sheep and was brought up by them. The lion cub grew up, with the belief that it was actually a sheep and it showed all the signs and traits of being a sheep. Like any normal sheep it would follow all the others in the flock, it grazed in the fields on the grass that grew there and it behaved in a shy and timid manner, causing no trouble amongst the rest of the flock. A day came when an older, adult lioness discovered the flock of sheep and saw the lion cub in the midst of them. The cub had now grown into a healthy juvenile, far larger than any of the sheep that it was living with, but still with its gentle demeanour and still happy to be part of the flock.

The old lion waited and prowled around the edge of the flock, looking for the opportunity to make its move. Seizing the moment, in ran in to the centre of the flock and took the frightened cub by the scruff of its neck and removed it from its adopted family of sheep. The older lion then proceeded to take the cub to a nearby watering hole, where its reflection could be seen on the calm surface of the water. As the lions stood there gazing at their reflections, the younger of the two was seeing for the first time in his life, his true identity. As the realisation of who, and what he was slowly dawned on him, the sheepish fear and timidity was replaced by the boldness and courage of a lion, an experience and sensation that he had never before felt. From that day, the cub was no longer a sheep following the flock. He grew to be a strong, courageous lion. However, for the rest of his life he never once attacked or hunted any sheep, but rather felt a compassion and understanding towards them.

*

As I have journeyed through my life I have come to realise and to know, that I am not what others have decided that I am. All the labels that have been attached to me, all the projected perceptions of who I am, all the burdens of expectation that have been placed upon me, these are not who I am. I am not a sheep, I am not a label. I am far more than that.

I am not my history

Having spent much of the time over the last few years of my life writing and teaching about Stillness, and living in and enjoying the present moment, the now, it may seem strange for me to be writing a book about the past. But I recognize that if it were not for the past there would be no present.

There is absolutely nothing wrong in acknowledging the past, and appreciating the fact that it is all the things that have happened in our own personal past that has led us to where we are in the present moment. The most important thing with regard to the past is to allow it to go, to be able to leave it behind and not try to continue to live in it. By all means, look back at the past on occasions, and remember what it is that has made you what you are today. Appreciate all those lessons that you have learnt, the people that have come and gone in your life, the places that have played a part in your journey so far, and dwell in the present, the present that has been created by your past.

I don't long for the past, for those times that you will read about as I share my memories and my journey. I don't look back and wish that it were like it was in the old days, the days of my youth. I look back and give thanks for every moment that has brought me to where I am now.

I have written this book whilst sitting at various tables and on different sofas over a period of months. One time, sitting at the kitchen table, on a December day, in a beautiful old cottage in the grounds of Prinknash Abbey, a Benedictine Monastery in the Gloucestershire countryside of England. Another time in a different cottage on a Spring day at Aberglasney Gardens in South West Wales. Yet other chapters have been written at home, in the peaceful surroundings of the Gower peninsula. Each time I have sat with my lap-top, a life full of memories and lessons learnt, and a grateful heart.

The Law of Karma

I think that it is important to first clarify what is meant by the term, *"The Law of Karma"*. There is so much misunderstanding, misconception, and erroneous teaching surrounding the subject of Karma that it is probably best that we establish what it is not.

Karma, as I understand it, has nothing to do with judgment, retribution and punishment. We often hear words spoken such as, *"Karma will come back and get him/her for those actions"*, as if there is some unseen force that sits in judgment ready to deal out punishment for any wrongdoing one may have done, or to reward one for all the acts of goodness and kindness. This is such a false idea of what Karma is all about. If this were so, then we would not see those who walk over others, and treat them badly, doing so well in life and being rewarded with comfortable lives of luxury. Neither would we see those who live a life of service and dedication to others suffering illness, hardship and poverty.

What has the little child who is dying of cancer done that was so bad that they deserve such Karma? Why is the multi-national financier who has exploited and trodden under foot so many on his way to the top, rewarded with such a good life and material benefits? Do you really believe that those suffering in war-torn countries, famine hit areas and natural disasters deserve what is happening to them because it is their Karma? And if so, why bother to help them if that is the way it is meant to be? It is the belief of many that this judgmental form of Karma carries forward from previous life-times, that what happens in this life is a result of the Karma built up in a past life. Were this to be the truth, then we have no right to interfere when somebody is suffering or being hurt, as this is simply what their present-life Karma is dictating – it's what they deserve. If someone is raped or murdered, do we just shrug our shoulders and say, *"that was their Karma"*? Should we just accept the fact and turn a blind eye to the rapist or murderer because they were simply delivering the Karma to their victims?

Of course not. That would be ridiculous. As far as I am concerned it would be as ridiculous as the idea of a loving god who would condemn his children, who do not behave as he wants, to an eternity of hell-fire and damnation. My understanding of God, Spirit, Source Energy, Divine Mind, Universe or whatever you want to call it, is that it is a benign, compassionate, loving energy and not some judgmental being sitting on a throne in heaven ready to wield a big stick whenever we step out of line.

The Sanskrit word *"karma"* means action, work or deed; it also refers to the spiritual principle of cause and effect where intent and actions of an individual (cause) influence the future of that individual (effect).

My view of the law of Karma is purely that and nothing else. According to ancient teachings, it is simply the law of cause and effect. Every action, every inaction, every word, even every thought has a resulting outcome. This book is the effect of me sitting down at my lap-top and typing in the words, which in turn came from the "cause" of me getting out of bed this morning. The fact that I got out of bed this morning comes from the action of me getting into bed last night. We can trace back everything that is happening now to all the things that have happened in our lives, and the lives of our ancestors, and their ancestors in the past. This is the Law of Karma, the law of cause and effect.

I must stress that what I am talking about here is my own personal view, which although shared by many, would not be the view of those who see Karma as a judgmental law of punishment and reward. I believe that the way Karma is most often viewed is as a result of religious organisations and institutions instilling fear in people to *"conform or be punished"*. The instilling of the fear of God has diverted from the original true meaning, which is the natural law of cause and effect.

The following accounts of incidents, situations, people and life experiences are all linked together by the law of Karma. One thing has led to another, and to another, and to another, until I have come to this present moment. Karma does not always work in a straight line however. There are junctions and forks where the karmic road divides, but when we trace those roads back we will always discover the causes along the way that have led us to where we are now. This doesn't just apply to our own lives, but to the lives of everybody else who has been affected by our actions, words and decisions, in the same way that our lives are affected by the actions, words and decisions of others.

My first intention in writing this book is not for you to blame yourselves, or anyone else for that matter, for things that have happened in the past, but simply to understand that everything in your historical past, in my historical past, even in the historical past of the whole world, has brought us to where we are in this present moment. There is no blame or judgment, that would be fruitless, just gratitude, awareness and understanding.

My second intention is for you to realise your uniqueness, your individuality, your place in the bigger picture of life, and above all, to realise your true, perfect self.

Early Memories

My earliest memories are really just a collection of random moments that have no particular story behind them, but together they seem to come from a place of safety and security. I remember very clearly sitting in my high chair as a toddler, eating the food that had been set before me. I'm guessing, that due to the fact that I was in a high chair, I would have been around 18 months to 2 years old at the time. If I close my eyes now, I can still feel the texture of the wooden chair and, somewhat bizarrely, the taste of the wood. I remember my pushchair and being pushed into town on a Saturday afternoon, and a little later I can remember the leather reins that I wore, which my Dad held onto as we walked through the shops, watching the shop assistants behind the dairy counter in Sainsbury's as they used the wooden paddles to pat the butter into blocks. I also have clear memories of my mother taking me for walks in the park.

Moving forward a little bit, I again have a really vivid memory of sitting on my mother's lap, feeling safe as she cuddled me. The rain beating on the window, the open coal fire roaring in the grate and hearing the words, *"Are you sitting comfortably? Then I'll begin"*, coming out of the speaker of the old valve wireless set as we listened to the BBC and *"Listen With Mother"* followed by *"Woman's Hour"*. I can also clearly remember sitting in the child's-seat on the back of my Dad's pushbike.

I don't remember my first day at St Mary's Church of England Primary School, but I do remember during that first year there, when I was just four years old, that we always had an afternoon nap in the classroom. Rows of wooden and canvas camp beds would be set out and all the first year pupils would lie down and sleep for half an hour. I'm still not entirely sure whether this was to give us, or the teacher, a rest for the afternoon.

There seems to be a pattern emerging here that involves sitting and lying down, could this be a precursor of my present day involvement with "*Stillness*".

I can also remember my parents, on a Sunday afternoon, standing in front of the fireplace, having a cuddle and kissing each other, much to my embarrassment.

All of these memories bring back a feeling of warmth, a feeling of being kept safe. The warmth and safety of being in my striped pyjamas, red dressing-gown and hugging a hot-water bottle as I was put to bed each night.

*

My parents, Trevor Reeves and Violet Hancock, both came from Swansea - where I myself now live, having moved here at the age of 17 when I left home to make my own way in the world.

Vi and Trev, as family and friends knew them, were married in 1943 and set up home in Kettering, Northamptonshire. After 4 years of enjoying and getting used to married life, Violet became pregnant, which resulted in the birth of their daughter, Glenys. Sadly, Glenys died when she was only 9 months old in 1948. I can't imagine what it must be like to lose a child, it seems to go totally against the way things should be. We all expect our parents to die before us, but to have a child die at such a young age is an experience that none of us ever dream of having to go through. The death of their daughter had a lasting effect on my parents, which stayed with them up until their own deaths many years later.

Although Glenys was born and died some years before I came along, she was always part of our family. Mum and Dad talked about her, her framed picture, which now hangs in my own cottage, had pride of place on the sideboard in the living room. Every April I would go along with my Dad to put flowers on her grave, although I have no recollection of Mum ever coming with us. I guess it was just too hard for her to face going to that little patch of ground at London Road Cemetery, with all the memories and broken dreams, reinforcing the hurt of never being able to witness her little girl growing up into adulthood. All the dreams that one has when a child is born, of watching them grow up and develop their own personalities, going through school, all the worries and joys as they go through their teenage years and start to develop relationships, maybe going on to have families of their own, dreams that would never be fulfilled for my mother.

The knowledge that I have a sister, even though I never met her, has had a great influence on my life, and continues to do so to this day. I feel so sure that one day, when my own life comes to an end, that I will meet with her and know her as my sister. I once wrote and recorded a song for her:

Candle In The Night

Once there was an angel who came down to spend some time on earth,
I never knew her but she taught me what life was worth.
She was like a Candle in The Night,
Light shining so bright

I never met her, she only stayed for a while,
But I saw her picture, and I saw her smile.

Every day of my life I know she's been by
my side
One day when I meet her with my arms
open wide
I'm gonna tell her that I've loved her,
She's always been on my mind
And we'll finally be together
When I leave these things behind.

She was like a Candle in The Night,
Light shining so bright
Like a Candle in The Night
Sweet sister, my sweet sister.

At the time of my sister's death, which was not long after the end of the Second World War, my parents didn't have the money to have a memorial stone placed on Glenys's grave, and so she was buried without a marker. My parents were members of The Salvation Army and, tragically, around the same time, the Salvation Army Officers in Kettering also lost their baby son. Garth Davidson lies in a grave next to my sister, and his memorial stone is the only way that I have ever been able to locate the resting place of Glenys. The following passage is taken from my first book, *Be Still,* and describes the day when I went to Glenys's grave in 1993 to spend some time talking to her and offering our mother back after so many years.

One of the things that my mother had decided
was that she wanted to be cremated and,

25

believing that her body was simply a vehicle for her soul to inhabit in this life, had no particular preference as to what should be done with her ashes. Dad decided that Mum's ashes should be scattered at the crematorium. A few days after the funeral a thought came to me, too late to do anything about now though, that it would have been nice to have scattered her ashes on my sister's grave. I decided to visit my sister's grave as I felt I wanted to say to her "look, we've had the joy of having Mum around all these years, and thank you for that, now it's your turn to be reunited with her".

I had a vague idea of where she was buried so knowing that she was buried next to another young child whose name was Garth, who did have a memorial stone where he lay, all I had to do was to locate Garth's grave and I would then find Glenys'. This was easier said than done, I don't know how many graves there are in Kettering cemetery but after nearly an hour of fruitless searching I was just about ready to give up. I had been all around the area that I thought I remembered, I had even been around an area that seemed to be set aside for the final resting place of children but I had been unable to find a stone with Garth's name engraved on it.

As I was about to leave the cemetery and give up the search, something happened that to this day I have only ever shared with a handful of people. I'm not what you might call a "cat-

lover"; in fact throughout my life I have been plagued with an allergy to cats. I only have to be in a room where a cat has been and my throat starts to itch and my eyes start to water. Somehow, cats seem to sense this and make a decided effort to come and sit on my lap if ever I am in their company. As I started to make my way to the gate I noticed a cat starting to follow me, the cat then did something, which I don't think is very normal for cats to do. It started nipping at my trouser leg with its teeth. It pulled at my hem and then would move back a few paces and sit and look at me. It did this 3 or 4 times as if it wanted me to follow it. Thinking to myself "this is stupid", I followed the cat until it made itself comfortable and sat down on a grave. Was this it? Had this cat somehow led me to my sister's burial place? I went over to it and read the inscription on the stone and to my disappointment realised that it was not the one I had been searching for.

"This really is stupid", I said to myself and turned to leave. As I turned, there in front of me I read the name "Garth Davidson". I had found it and right alongside was a small, unmarked grave which was the resting place of my sister. I was able to say what I wanted to say and at the same time realise that my mother had not really gone. I believe that somehow either her spirit or energy, or that of my sister, had used that cat to guide me to where Glenys's body lay.

In 1949 my brother, Graham, came into the world, and I followed four years later in 1953 to complete the Reeves household and the moulding of my life as the youngest child of Violet & Trevor Reeves, began.

*

The late Dr Wayne W Dyer used to talk of how, for the first 9 months of our existence, God, or nature, takes care of things. Inside our mother's womb we are provided with all that we need for nourishment and for our growth, and our parents put their trust in this natural process. Then, when we are born, it is as if the parents say *"Ok, thank you god, you've done a great job, but we'll take over now."*

And so the conditioning begins.

We love to use labels in order to define what something, or someone, is. But it really doesn't matter what we name something, its essence doesn't change because we give it a name. Today, as I am writing this, my wife and I are enjoying a week long retreat from our usual day to day life and staying in a cottage in the grounds of Aberglasney Gardens in Carmarthenshire. Earlier on today I was enjoying looking at all the plants as we walked around the woodland area and also the landscaped gardens. I have no idea what most of the plants are called, either their Latin names or their common names, but that did not stop me enjoying them, their colours and shapes, their sizes and smells. I didn't need to label them in order to appreciate them. William Shakespeare was right when he wrote those now familiar words in Romeo & Juliet: *"What is in a name? That which we call a rose by any other word would smell as sweet"*

My birth certificate bears the name John Reeves. That's the name my parents gave me, the label that was put on me when I was born. That name was the first of many labels that would be placed upon me throughout my life. Son of Vi & Trev, naughty, show off, rebel, joker, trouble-maker, brother, husband, father, carer, musician, therapist, writer, teacher, and many others. The list is endless with some of them being warning-labels and others being a bit more positive, but labels none the less. When I became a professional musician I started to use the name Jim Fox, a name that I still use today. I have always known, yet it took me a long time to actually realise it, that I am not what the label put on me says that I am. I am not what other people want me to be, or expect me to be. I am not who you say I am.

There is a Zen teaching that says that when we let go of all that we know and all that we think we know, all the things that have been given to us by others, including our name and personality, instructions and morals, our lessons and understanding, we become once again as pure and innocent as a new-born child. This is, what I believe was, one of the meanings behind what Jesus was talking about when he said; *"You must be born-again"*. Unless we are stripped of all the layers that we have been clothed with by others, we cannot discover who we truly are.

Who am I then?

29

It is one thing to know who one is not, but it has taken me a long time to know who I am. It has been a journey that has taken over 60 years so far, and which still continues today. It has been a journey that has led to a stripping down of all the layers that have built up over those years. I do understand however, that every single thing, every word spoken, every action taken, every turning made throughout my life has led me to this point, this moment that I am now in, and this understanding of who I am. As I pointed out at the beginning, this book is an account of that journey.

*

Rather than trying to describe my journey in chronological terms, I have attempted to split it into categories. Each category is a journey in itself, travelling a separate path. Although there are times when two or three paths may meet and cross over, I hope that the reader will find it more interesting if I set it out in this way.

School Days

Once we reach the age of 4 or 5, maybe younger for today's children, we spend as many hours if not more, in school or formal education, than we do with our families. A typical week for me would have involved spending 6 hours a day from Monday to Friday at school and maybe 4 hours at most with my family. As I got older and was expected to do homework, those 4 hours would start to get eaten into.

Weekends were not a lot different. A Sunday was a very full day for me having been brought up as a member of The Salvation Army, which often meant that even less family time could be enjoyed, as there was Sunday School and services to attend. Saturday was really the only day I would get to spend with Mum and Dad for any length of time, and even then, Dad would often be at work on a Saturday morning, then doing odd-jobs around the house or in his shed, in the afternoon.

I can honestly say that I never really enjoyed going to school. Between the ages of 4 and 17 I attended 3 different educational institutions, and although there were some lessons and subjects that I took an interest in, it was never something that I looked forward to and I became expert at faking illnesses in order to spend a day at home with my own choice of books. If I complained of feeling unwell, my mother would put her hand on my forehead to check if my temperature was high. It didn't take long to discover that if I placed my warm hands on my head for a few minutes before calling for my mother, she would feel the heat and keep me at home for the day. I also suffered from asthma, which was something I could turn to my own advantage when needed. On those sick-days, I would actually enjoy watching the schools programmes on TV, choosing what subjects I was interested in. Seeing people acting out famous battles, or viewing a day in the life of a caveman on the TV history programmes was far more exciting than the endless list of dates that we got in the classroom. Right from those first days I think I felt that I was being taught what people wanted me to learn, rather than what I was interested in, or wanted to know about.

My first school, when I was 4 years old was St Mary's Church of England Primary School, on Fuller Street, in Kettering. It wasn't a large school, only one class per year. The classes themselves were big though, with one teacher being responsible for about 33 pupils. I don't remember too much about it, apart from the bits that actually stimulated me. I would enjoy the music and singing lessons, when we would sing along to Sea Shanties and old folk songs being broadcast on the BBC radio programme for schools. Songs like "Riding On A Donkey" and "Blow The Man Down". It was also fun to make a noise with the tambourines, drums and castanets in what was deceptively known as the school band. Hard though it might be for people who know me now, to believe, I also used to enjoy the weekly country dancing class, when we would all assemble in the school hall and be partnered up to dance to such tunes as the Cumberland Reel. I'm sure that my enthusiasm had nothing to do with the little blonde-haired girl that I usually had to hold hands with as my dancing partner. Music was to play an important part in my future life, but dancing, I'm afraid, was not.

My interest in the theatre was fuelled by the occasional visit to the school by educational theatre companies. I don't remember anything about the productions other than that they always seemed to involve stepladders! Each Christmas we would take part in the school nativity play, which we performed in St Mary's Church. I played various parts including the inn-keeper, a shepherd and one of the wise-men. My ambition though, to play the role of Joseph, was never realised. I remember clearly, those dark evenings going along to the church, and changing into costume in the cold vestry. I enjoyed so much the idea of playing a role, taking on a different persona and being seen in a different light.

Strange as it may seem for a Church of England school, May Day played an important part in the school calendar, with its symbolic pagan fertility dance around the Maypole, of which as seven year olds we had absolutely no understanding. The weeks leading up to the May Day festivities involved a lot of practice of the complicated dances around the pole, but it was a welcome relief from the drudgery of lessons as the May Queen and her attendants were chosen and the pageantry took place in the schoolyard.

When I was about 10 years old, we had a new

headmaster in the junior department of the school. Peter Findlay was a keen amateur actor and member of the local amateur dramatics group in Kettering. Apart from Miss Mona Bailey, who was my first teacher in the infants, Mr Findlay was a teacher that I actually liked. Not so much for his teaching skills, but because of his stories of his theatrical exploits. Once, when he was undertaking the role of Fagin in Lionel Bart's Oliver, he stood in front of the class and entertained us with a rendition of "*You've Got To Pick A Pocket Or Two*", much to the delight of all the children.

There was one occasion, after he had been on a trip to the West End in London to see a production of Auden's *Brief Lives* when he enthusiastically told us of how when the audience walked into the auditorium, the actor was already seated on the stage in the setting of his study, seemingly asleep, ready to wake up when everyone was seated and the lights went down. I've never actually seen a performance of the play, but the wonderfully clear picture that Mr Findlay painted in my mind's eye has stayed with me to this day.

In *Brief Lives*, Auden recounts his memories of famous, and not so famous, characters and contemporaries, one of these being Sir Walter Raleigh. Looking back, I'm not so sure how appropriate it was for our Headmaster to relate to a class of 10 and 11 year olds the scene where Auden speaks of Sir Walter Raleigh. At the height of a moment of passion, the young lady with whom Raleigh was entangled is calling out "Sweet Sir Walter, sweet Sir Walter". Becoming lost in the moment of ecstasy, the words begin to slur and morph into "*Swisser Wasser, swisser Wasser.*" I certainly class Peter Findlay as being one of my inspirations in life, and I still own a copy of Auden's *Brief Lives* to this day.

Exams were a big part of the school year. Each June, we would have to sit an exam and somehow, I always managed to do fairly well. I would usually finish in the top 3 in my class. I'm not quite sure how this happened, there were subjects that I was particularly keen on and always did well in, such as English and Spelling and also basic Arithmetic, but when it came to Geography and remembering what the average rainfall was in Patagonia, I was simply not interested. Back in 1964, all pupils had to sit their 11-plus examinations when they reached the age of 11. The results of these exams would determine which secondary school you would go to. If you passed the 11-plus you were accepted for the Grammar School, if you were borderline you could then go on for an individual interview, which again, if passed, would gain you access to the Grammar School, or entrance to what was known as The Central School. Failure to pass meant that you would be condemned to the Secondary Modern School; an awful system, which our present UK government is trying to reinstate even as I write.

Four years before me, my brother Graham had secured an interview and was accepted to be a pupil at Kettering Grammar School. This achievement was to cause me a lot of grief during this period. I was constantly being compared to my brother, who spent so much of his time studying in order to gain the grades necessary to progress towards the Grammar School. I would hear the words, "*Why can't you be more* like Graham?" and *"If you don't do your homework, you'll be good for nothing and end up as a street cleaner or dustman"*. In my mind, expecting a child to spend 6 hours a day in lessons at school and then to come home and spend another 2 or 3 hours doing homework was simply not fair. Added to that was the fact that maybe only a couple of pupils from my school each year would go on to the Grammar School, which meant that most of my friends would be going to the Secondary Modern School and I wanted to be with them, rather than being like my brother. I was not, and am not, my brother, so to try to be like him would be pointless and would also be denying who I am. There is nothing wrong with whom my brother is, I have total respect for him and what he has done with his life, and I love him dearly. To try and mould my life into what is already the life of someone else is something that I learnt at a young age, was simply pointless and futile. I remember a famous English entertainer and impersonator called Mike Yarwood, who had a very popular show on television in which he mimicked various other entertainers and politicians of the day. At the end of his show he would move from his impressions to being himself with the words *"and this . . . is me"*. I can look at those whom I admire, or who inspire me and know that that is them, but this is me.

I took my 11-plus examinations with the intention of failing. What a curious, and hurtful word that can be - failure. For me it wasn't failure, because I got the result that I set out to achieve, but for so many that concept can condemn and destroy. To be told that they are failures is to take away hope and dignity. The fear and stigma of failure was something that I would have to face at various times during the years to come. Much to the disappointment of my parents I left St Mary's C of E School and became a student at Stamford Road Secondary School for Boys. It was a school that at the time did not have a particularly good reputation.

During the four years I spent at Stamford Road I had little interest in school life, apart from English lessons and the rare occasions when the school would get involved in putting on a drama production. On the whole, they were miserable years for me. Apart from one temporary Maths teacher, there wasn't one other member of staff that I could say I liked, or who inspired me. There were a couple that I did end up feeling sorry for, as we did give them a hard life and, although not being one of the ringleaders, I did play my part in making their lives hell. My third year at Stamford Road, was probably the worst. 3B was the class that had a reputation, during that school year we saw 3 science teachers try and fail to teach us anything - one of them gave up teaching altogether and went to work in a petrol station a few hundred yards away from the school. Not the best move that he could have made, as his presence there did attract more than a few mocking visits from some of his former pupils.

I don't think that we were a class of particularly bad boys, and we certainly weren't stupid or unintelligent. It was simply that we were bored and frustrated. Lessons were by no means interactive, the teachers stood at the front of the class and rattled off information, facts, figures, dates etc., but there was no life in the words, there was no fire or passion. It felt like, as students, we were being pushed along a conveyor belt with bits of information applied to us as we went along, until eventually we would all come out at the end as the product the school intended us to be. Well, I was having none of that. I would not be put into a mould and manufactured. That was not who I was. Labels were slapped on me, school reports put me down, teachers and parents tried to control me and make me into what they wanted rather than finding out what I wanted. I don't remember ever once being seriously asked by anyone, what I wanted to do with my life. I was in total rebellion, not understanding why on earth I was being taught such things as logarithms, technical drawing, woodwork, metalwork, and other things that I knew then, and rightly so, that I would never actually put to use in my life. My frustration at not being given the opportunity to be myself or to discover what it was that I wanted for my life would boil over and deprive me of the joy that could have been there for me.

A short period of relief from this feeling of emptiness and pointlessness would come during my final year at Stamford Road School, when somebody came up with the brilliant idea of a joint dramatic production between our school and Rockingham Road School, the local Girls' Secondary School. As you can probably imagine, a very large number of pupils from an all-boys school would be keen to audition for a part in a play that would involve real live girls. I was one of the fortunate ones to be given a part in our production of Bertolt Brecht's *The Caucasian Chalk Circle*, mainly because I had recently bought my first guitar and was able to play a grand total of 4 chords to accompany the character of *The Singer*, who was the narrator of the tale. I remember the feeling as I came out onto the stage of the hall, at the girls' school, for the first rehearsal, picking out the notes of Chopin's Funeral March. With this came the revelation of the magnetic powers of being able to play the guitar, I had never been so popular, and that night I got to walk home the best looking girl in the play. This joint production of *The Caucasian Chalk Circle* was to be my first public outing as a guitarist - the first of many in the years to come.

At the age of 15, it was time to leave Stamford Road School and to make some decisions. I had really enjoyed being part of the theatrical production and decided that I wanted to go to Drama School. I wrote off to a number of different institutions, requesting a prospectus and to find out what, if any, qualifications I would need to be eligible for enrolment. This was a time when all one needed to be accepted to a Teacher Training College was 5 O-levels, so I wasn't expecting the requirements to be too high. I looked through each prospectus as it arrived and decided on a couple that I would like to apply for. I told my parents what I had in mind, and that proved to be the end of that particular dream. The message was clear, that going to Drama College was a ridiculous idea and I needed to decide on getting a proper job, one that would give me some stability and security. I didn't exactly get any help or direction from my parents as to what would be an acceptable career choice, but they just made it clear that acting was something I should forget. The careers advisor at school was equally unhelpful; all he could say was to choose a job wisely as it would be something that I would be doing for the next 50 years until I retired. What a different world we lived in then! That was nearly 50 years ago and you will read later in this book that it has been slightly more than one job that has occupied my time in those years.

One thing that I had always enjoyed doing was writing, at both primary and secondary school I had put together very basic school magazines with short stories, articles and puzzles. I got great pleasure, not just from writing the magazines, but also from putting them together and designing the layout. Writing stories was something that seemed to come naturally to me and mostly I would get good marks for my compositions. There was one story however that got me into trouble and resulted in me getting 'six of the best' with the cane across my backside. If I remember rightly it involved a milkman and a lonely customer. My English teacher told me that if he wanted to read rubbish like that he could buy a cheap paperback from the corner shop. At the time, I took his comment as a compliment.

At school I had terrible handwriting, something that has never really improved throughout my life. Maybe this was the reason I had wanted to own my own typewriter, so that I would actually be able to read what I had written. The thought occurred to me that it might be a good idea to learn to type - but that was something that girls did. I then discovered that the local Technical College offered a course in Business Studies, which involved learning to touch-type, as well as such useful skills as book-keeping and accounting, and commerce. On leaving secondary school I applied for a place at Kettering Technical College and in September 1968 I embarked on my Business Studies course, adding on the subjects of English Language, English Literature, Religious Education and History.

Life at the Tech was so different to that in school. No longer a pupil, I was now a student. It felt like I had grown up. Students were treated differently, the school uniform was discarded, and I was able to wear what I wanted. This in itself was a liberation of expression. It was the era of the hippy - flowers, flares and freedom. It was a real awakening for me as I made new friends, discovered new and exciting things about the world and was allowed to develop my own opinions. For the first time in my life it felt like people were actually listening to me and taking notice of me as an individual. My tastes in music and reading material developed and expanded and some of the chains that I felt had been restricting me, started to fall away. Added to that, I was finally learning something that would be of use to me for the rest of my life. I would look forward to the touch-typing class that I would attend 4 times a week, not just because I found it so liberating, but also because I was one of only 2 boys amongst a group of 20 girls! Nearly 50 years later and I am still employing that skill as I type these words on my laptop.

I made the most of the first year at Kettering Tech, leaning the things that I wanted to learn and getting good qualifications to go along with the new skills. The problems started to come during the second year when the boredom crept in again. I had reached a good standard in typing, I could put together basic small business accounts and gained a handful of O level

General Certificate of Education passes along with a few other qualifications - what more did I need? I was beginning to enjoy the social side of being a student far more than the educational side and lost interest in what was the sub-text of Shakespeare's Hamlet, or what Alexander Pope was really trying to say through his poetry. I wanted to be able to enjoy a play or a book for what it was, rather than dissecting it to find hidden meaning. In time, I stopped attending classes and lectures and spent more time in the student common room, or local cafés. I'm sure I learnt more by exchanging views with my fellow students, and discovering things for myself, than I ever did in a stuffy classroom or lecture hall being force-fed text book mechanics. From that moment a normal college day would start at 9.00 am at the café above Fine Fare Supermarket on the High Street, and then we would cross the road to the Wimpy Bar when it opened at 10.00 am. After that we would head back to the college common room for lunch before going back into town to play skittles in one of the local pubs.

I finished my full-time education in June 1970 having learnt much, but not necessarily in the way it had been intended. Childhood is such a precious time and should not be used by adults to indoctrinate and replicate. I truly believe that we should encourage young people to learn through experience and that that experience should be theirs and not the experience of others. The education system should not be a sausage machine, churning out replicas or clones of those who teach; rather it should be a means of helping the student to develop their own unique individuality and to follow the path of their choosing. Children need to be taught the important things about how to live - respect, love, compassion, sharing, responsibility for their actions, stewardship of the earth and care of the environment. If, and when, they show an interest in other subjects, they will want to learn about them, but the idea that all this education has to be crammed into such a short period of time, and that certain levels should be reached by specific ages, has the tendency to take away from the child the joy of childhood. The number of under 18 year olds committing suicide has grown over recent years, and it is my belief that the stress put on them to achieve, to pass exams and to gain qualifications has a great bearing on this. In today's education system when we test children throughout their school days, starting from the age of 4 or 5, we are simply adding to stress and pressure, surely this cannot be right.

At this stage in my life as I look back, I can see that the education system that I came through was not perfect and had many failings, but I am grateful for all of it. Everything that happened during those years was part of my Karma, each step was the result of the previous step, each effect was the direct result of the cause on my karmic journey. If it had not been for all that, I would not be sitting here writing these words at this moment in my life.

Family Life

It is all too easy to dwell on the negative things in life, to focus on the problems, and to remember the not too pleasant times. Just as a painter steps away from the canvas to appreciate and to evaluate his work, so too we need to step back to see the whole picture of our lives.

While I was growing up I found lots to complain about with regards to my home and family. My brother and I didn't really get on too well when we were younger, we were both so different, he was quiet and studious and, to my mind, far too serious, whereas I was totally the opposite. I was loud, a bit of an extrovert, some would say a show-off, which now if I'm honest, I would have to agree with. I certainly wasn't studious when it came to school work, although I did love to read about the things that interested me, and when I got my first guitar I would spend hours learning how to tune it and how to play my first chords. Although we didn't have much in common, and our lives took off in totally different directions, I am grateful for the fact that Graham has always been there for me, and there have been times in my life when I have really needed that support from him - he has never let me down. We don't have a massive amount of contact with each other, meeting only occasionally at family celebrations or funerals or if one of us happens to be in the vicinity of the other's home, but I think that we both know that we are there for each other if needed.

I constantly locked horns with my father, whom I regarded as far too strict and quick to punish when I stepped out of line, or when I didn't match up to the expectations he had of me. We were probably too similar in many ways and were both afflicted with the curse of the redhead - our tempers were very short and easily ignited.

I really can't find anything negative to say about my mother, although I'm sure there must have been moments when she needed to display her authority in a firm way. All my memories of her are of her being a wonderful homemaker and mum. She made sure that she was always there when I came home from school, meals were always on the table, the house was always clean, and the front step was always scrubbed. I mentioned before that one of my earliest memories is of sitting on her lap, listening to the wireless, and that's how I remember her - full of love and laughter. Oh yes, the laughter, Mum had a wonderfully infectious laugh and there was a lot of laughter when she was around. So much so that when my grandfather died, the sight and sound of her sitting at the dining room table with tears running down her face as she cried for the loss of her dad, was such a piercing blow to me as a 5 year old. It wasn't the loss of my Poppa that hurt, but seeing the pain that my mother was experiencing.

Many years later, I now realise and appreciate how blessed I was to have such a wonderful family. My parents were never what you might call well-off, Dad had to work hard for everything that we had. The small two-bedroom house we lived in was well looked after and was always in good repair. Every year we were able to go away on holiday, sometimes we managed to fit two in. We had family in South Wales and also on the South coast of England, so sometimes we were able to stay with relatives, other times it would be in a caravan somewhere and we even got to stay in a guest-house in Folkestone in Kent on a couple of occasions. During the visits to Kent we were regaled with stories of Dad's war-time service as he guarded the Romney Marshes against the prospect of Hitler gaining entry to our green and pleasant land. It was in Kent that Dad picked up his "war-wound" when the jeep he was travelling in had to brake suddenly and the butt of his rifle, which was between his legs, hit him on his head!

As a young child, probably the biggest fault that I had was that I was unable to recognise where a line needed to be drawn. So often I was told off for "*not knowing when to stop*" or for "*going too far*". As I've already mentioned, I was a bit of a show-off and liked to be the centre of attention. If there was a joke to be played, I would be there to play it, the trouble was I would usually try to stretch the joke out far after it had stopped being funny. It must have been particularly hard for my parents on April 1st each year when I would be playing all sorts of April Fool's jokes, when they would have been remembering the anniversary of my sister's death. I remember getting up very early one year, having a bought a special pen from the joke shop with which I then went around the house making marks that resembled cracks on anything glass. The windows, Television and mirrors all looked like they had been smashed.

Being easily excitable and also suffering from childhood asthma, I don't remember many birthday parties or Christmas gatherings where I didn't have to end up going to bed early, either because I had overstepped the mark or because I had managed to bring on an asthma attack. Sunday tea-times were always guaranteed to see me getting into trouble, particularly if other family members had been invited round to join us. Whenever I meet up with my cousin, Stuart, he is quick to remind me of the Sunday afternoon battles. I don't know what it was, but there was just something about these gatherings that brought out the worst in me and I would end up arguing with my Dad and, inevitably, being sent off to bed.

One occasion when I failed to listen, and managed to push it that little bit too far was during a family outing to Wicksteed Park. Well before the days of Alton Towers and suchlike, Wicksteed Park, in Kettering, was one of the main leisure facilities in England. Family outings were common events; uncles, aunts, cousins and extended family members would often get together on a bank holiday for a picnic and games. During one particular gathering we were playing cricket in the park when my brother, Graham, was batting and I was fielding. I don't remember how many times I was told not to stand so close to the batsman, but I didn't listen to any of the warnings, resulting in Graham taking a swing at the ball and whacking me over the head with his bat, just above my right eye. I still have the scar where I had to be stitched up by the medics. I should point out here that he didn't intentionally hit me with the cricket bat, it was entirely my fault. Karma in action, I was the cause and I felt the effect.

My father worked hard, working five and a half days a week in a shoe factory and then taking on extra part-time work in the evenings. I do wish that he had been around more, and not worked so hard, but I also understand his reasons for working so hard. We may not have had the luxuries of some folk, but we never, ever, went without.

With all his hard work, and the tiredness that came with it, my teenage years put a particular strain on the relationship between Dad and myself. As I became more and more rebellious, kicking against authority and institution, his understanding of me grew weaker and we would often argue. Being of the old school which believed that corporal punishment was the only way to discipline a child, I would often feel 'the back of his hand', as he would put it, and sometimes the sting of his belt. Nowadays that would probably horrify some people, but back then life was a lot different and, although I am not advocating this form of discipline for children, I hold no ill feeling towards my father for the way he brought me up and, as many of my generation would say, it really didn't do me any harm.

At the age of 17, feeling frustrated and trapped at home, I decided it was time to leave and make my own life away from Kettering. I had met somebody during a holiday spent with family in Swansea and we had been writing to each other for a few months and, when we felt that the time was right, she set about finding some lodgings for me with a lovely, elderly couple called Mr & Mrs Hill. On Boxing Day 1970, I told my parents I was leaving home to go and live in Swansea. I had expected an argument from my Dad, but what actually happened was a huge shock to me.

I will never forget going into my parent's bedroom and finding my father lying on the bed crying his eyes out. He was really, really sobbing. There was no way that I had expected that, and for the first time in my life, Dad and I actually talked. Not just words but a real sharing of thoughts and emotions. He couldn't understand why I was leaving and wanted to know if it was something that he had done that was driving me away. I explained, as best I could, that I really needed to leave home, I needed to do it for me, to try to build my own life, to be the person that I was, not the person that others expected me to be. That conversation was the beginning of a healing process that was to take a long time to complete, and involve many more years of pain.

Graham had left home 3 years earlier, to go to a Teacher Training College in Coventry, and now that I had left home as well, to start my own life in Swansea, Mum and Dad were free to start living their lives as well. Instead of having to consider their children before doing anything, they now had a new liberty to follow their own path together. After a while, Dad gave up his job in the factory, they sold their house and bought a small guesthouse in Blackpool. This was something my Mum had always wanted to do, but the ties of a family had made this impossible in her mind. Although my leaving had caused initial pain, the karmic result of my actions meant that my parents were able to fulfil a dream.

My mother's sister and brother-in-law, Auntie Eileen and Uncle John, had moved to Blackpool a little while before and so Mum and Dad followed after them, taking my grandmother with them and finding a nice flat for her to live in and keep her independence. They took to their new lives like ducks to water. They were the perfect hosts and the guesthouse was a great success. Mum did what she did best - she provided a homely atmosphere for the guests and made them welcome whilst she cooked them fantastic breakfasts. Dad fell into his role with no problem at all, keeping the guests entertained and happy, they were both happier than they had ever been and both of them said that they wished they had done it years before. This was a lesson in following your dreams in the moment, rather than waiting and wasting precious time.

I meet so many people these days who don't follow their dreams, their passion for what they know in their hearts they should be doing. When I saw how happy my parents were in their new life, I too wished that they had done it earlier. What a waste it is for anyone to sacrifice their own dreams for the sake of others when that sacrifice can also be the cause of suffering and pain to those that you are trying to help and protect. I learnt a valuable and precious lesson at that time, one that would prove to be so important in my own life when I had to make a decision that involved my own children.

Just a couple of years after my parents moved to

Blackpool, their world was turned upside down. Dad started to experience strange blackouts, sometimes he would physically collapse, other times his mind would go blank and he would forget where he was or how he got there. On one occasion the police were called when he was found wandering quite a long way from home, not knowing anything about what he was doing there or where he was going to or coming from. He was eventually diagnosed with a form of osteoarthritis. A bone growth at the top of his spine was blocking the blood flow to his brain when he turned his head from side to side. Still a relatively young man in his mid-fifties he was forced to give up the guest house, forfeit his ability to drive a car, something that had always given him great pleasure, and move back to Kettering. For a few years following his diagnosis he had to wear a surgical collar, 24 hours a day, to stop his head moving quickly and bringing on a blackout. This was a particularly hard period for my mother, as Dad's personality was severely affected for some time, which resulted in a great deal of pressure being placed on my Mum. I too found it very difficult during the times that I would visit them for a few days. I really didn't understand the seriousness of his condition and when his already short temper fuse would ignite, I would react and we would end up having the most blazing of arguments, particularly when it seemed to me that my mother was on the receiving end of his mood changes. Whatever happened, and whatever was said, Mum wouldn't hear anything said against him, and stood by, supporting him through what was a very trying time. After one particular incident, Dad and I ended up crying together, we were both apologising to each other and both of us were telling the other that we loved them. Although we had probably said the words when I was a young child, I don't remember ever telling him that I loved him before, and I have no other memory of him saying the same to me. He was now over 70 years of age and I was getting closer to being 40. Nobody should ever allow themselves to reach such a point without saying those magical and powerful words to a parent or child, and as I write this I am all too aware that I don't tell my two daughters anywhere near enough, that I love them with my whole being.

Things eventually settled down as Dad's condition was brought under control. At least they had managed to have that time, short though it was, running their guesthouse with all the joy and satisfaction that it brought. Now they were able to begin to enjoy their retirement years together, often going on holiday with my Mum's sister Eileen and her husband John. The two couples had been inseparable throughout their married lives, spending much time together, and living within close proximity of each other. When Uncle John died, as a result of a car accident, Aunty Eileen moved into the same sheltered housing complex that Mum and Dad had moved into, just two years before. She continued living there until the wonderful age of 92 when she had to move into a care home due to her failing health. I try to visit her as often as I can, although it was always a bit of a strange feeling when I had to pass the front door of my parents' old flat in order to reach hers.

*

I have a belief that there is nothing in itself that is

either good or bad, but it is how we deal with it that makes it so. There are drugs that when used for purely selfish reasons can be totally destructive, whereas the same drug can be used to save someone's life. A car driven by a responsible person to get from one point to another is a useful and beneficial thing. The same car driven by the same person under the influence of alcohol, or perhaps in a temper can be turned into a lethal weapon. It is not the drug or the car that is good or bad, but how it is used and what is done with it.

Just a short time before their Golden Wedding Anniversary, both my parents were diagnosed, within two weeks of each other, with different forms of terminal cancer. News of my parents' cancer could have been seen as a devastating tragedy and a totally negative period in their lives, but we were all able to see so much positivity in the situation and to embrace it and allow it to enrich our lives in a way that nothing else could have done. During those final months that they had together, we became closer than I had ever known before. Mum took the news with such grace and acceptance, she knew that she was going to die and set about making it as easy for everyone as she possibly could. She kept laughing right up until the moment when she was under so much pain-control medication, that she was no longer able to communicate. As both my brother and I lived in different parts of the country, and my father was also living with his cancer, we worked together to make sure that we could be around as much as possible to care for them. At the time, Graham was headmaster of a school near London so he was only able to be with my parents at weekends. In contrast, I was able to see to it that most of my work as a musician and entertainer, took place at weekends, so I arranged to stay in Kettering during the week, whilst Graham would come up from his home at weekends.

Dad was still able to be mobile and active while Mum grew weaker and more tired. We had the wonderful support of the Community Nursing team and the MacMillan Nurses, this enabled Mum to be able to stay at home for as long as she wanted. A new hospice had recently opened, just across the road from their sheltered housing apartment, and Mum had made it clear to us that when she was ready she would let us know and she was to be taken over to the Cransley Hospice ward. In the meantime, she set about putting everything in order, passing on pieces of jewellery to her four granddaughters and ensuring that we knew where everything was. She also spent her last weeks preparing her own funeral service, choosing the hymns and readings that she wanted so that nobody needed to worry about anything.

When the time finally came, and she was ready to be moved over the road to the hospice, she let us know, as she said she would do, and arrangements were put into place and her care was put into the hands of Dr John Smith and his fantastic team of nurses and carers. The atmosphere on the Cransley ward was beautiful; peaceful, gentle music was being played on the cassette player and the care she received was so attentive. It was coming up to the weekend and I had some work commitments that I had to honour, so, not knowing if I was going to be able to see her again, we talked for a while, I kissed her and she laughed, and I told her that I would see her next week.

When I returned to Kettering after the weekend, Mum was much weaker and under sedation, unable to communicate and showing no signs that she knew anyone was there. One of the nurses told us that it would not be much longer, and that night, Dad and I sat by her bed keeping vigil. Graham stayed in Kettering and went to get some sleep in Mum & Dad's flat. At some point during the night, Mum's breathing started to show the signs that the end was very near. I phoned my brother to tell him to come back over and then went back to the bedside to be with Mum and Dad. It was then that the most wonderful thing happened. As I sat holding her hand, and Dad sat next to me, she opened her eyes and looked directly at me and mouthed the word "goodbye", and with that she took her final breath and left her body.

Death and dying were things that I had never had to deal with before, as children it was something that we had been shielded from. I remember my grandfather dying and the occasions when some elderly neighbour in the street had died, but it had never been as close as it was now. Because of that shielding there had always been a fear, I suppose it was the fear of the unknown, but that experience, that privilege of being with my mother in her final moments and seeing the look of peace on her face, marked the moment when I knew I would never again be afraid of dying. It may sound strange to some people, but being there as she left this life was the most beautiful and wonderful experience I have ever had in my life, and I treasure it dearly. It is something I would not have missed for the world.

I felt that I wanted to speak at Mum's funeral, but at the time I don't think I would have been able to get the words out without breaking down. I wrote down the words that I wanted to say and I recently came across them whilst going through some old papers. It may be over 20 years too late, but I would like to share them here.

The last few weeks have been, for all of us who came in contact with Mum during that time, both an inspiration and a lesson in the joy of life.

From the moment that Mum learnt of her illness, right through to the end, there was no word of complaint, no questioning "why?", no looking for, or wanting sympathy. In fact, the opposite was true; her faith told her to be glad and she was telling us how lucky she was that she wouldn't have to suffer like so many others do.

On many occasions during the last weeks, Mum told us that she didn't want us to be sad for her, she was happy. She knew where she was going and she wanted us to be happy for her.

Being with Mum as she was getting things sorted out, choosing the songs and readings in readiness for her funeral, making sure we knew where everything was and leaving instructions as to all that she wanted doing, has been a privilege that will never be forgotten.

I have a lifetime of memories of Mum, of the joys and the sadnesses we've been through over the years as a family, but I'm sure the longest lasting memory will be of her strength and faith these last weeks of her life. I will remember that wonderful laugh that we still heard right up until the last days, and also the selfless love that kept her caring for everybody else before she worried about her own problems.

It is impossible for us not to be sad today, because we have lost a very special person who means so much to all of us. But Mum wanted us to be happy and we can be happy. Not just because she is now enjoying peace, but also we can be happy because we have been allowed to share in the life of someone described by one of her neighbours as "A remarkable lady".

*

Dad had been dreading this moment; he and Mum had been together for over 50 years. They had experienced the joy of having children and the pain of losing one of those children. They had done everything together and had never been apart for more than a couple of days at a time. He didn't want to lose her; he wanted to be with her.

Dad had been diagnosed with Non-Hodgkin Lymphoma and, in a strange way this was a comfort to him, as he knew he wouldn't have to be without his beloved wife for long, as his days too, were few. A few days after Mum's funeral, I took Dad to see the consultant at Kettering General Hospital to get the results of some tests that had been carried out. On that visit we were told that the treatment he had been receiving had been successful and he was given the 'all clear'. Dad didn't want to hear this and refused to accept it. He kept saying *"But I've still got the cancer, haven't I?"* He had just lost his life's partner and his intention was to join her again as soon as possible, he had no will to be cured or to live without her.

The mind is an incredibly powerful thing, and I firmly believe, from my own experience, that the way we think about things can affect the things we think about. Using the energy of positive thoughts can help to bring about positive outcomes, and in the same way using the energy of negative thoughts can bring about negative outcomes. If you think like a victim, you are likely to experience being a victim. If an athlete thinks about being a victor, then he or she is likely to experience victory. My father wanted to be told that he still had cancer, he believed that he still had cancer and on the following visit, it was confirmed that he did indeed still have cancer. That was all that he wanted, he had no interest at all in facing a life on his own. During the next four months he had no joy in his life, he would sit for hours in a depressed state and turned in on himself. Mum had died in November, and that Christmas, Dad, who had always been the life-and-soul of the party with his joking and singing, just sat in the corner while everyone else tried to enter into the festive spirit. There was nothing that anyone could do in those months to help him or to bring some enjoyment into his life - he simply didn't want it.

Just like his beloved wife before him, he asked to be admitted to the Cransley Hospice ward as the cancer took hold and he began to fade away. Then, out of nowhere, he decided that he wanted to see his 75th birthday. He was very weak by now but we were able to arrange with the hospice and with the sheltered housing complex that had been his home for the last few years, for him to be wheeled back across the road in a wheelchair on the 15th March 1994, and be guest of honour at a birthday party being held for him in the communal lounge. Many friends and family came to celebrate with him and it was a brief moment of joy in his last days. It was also a form of closure for him. We took him back to the hospice after the party and he felt that he had achieved what he had wanted.

When we got him back into bed in the ward, there was another surprise waiting for him. One of the nurses had just returned from a couple of days off and had been on holiday in Cornwall. While she was there she visited an antique shop and noticed a collection of old coins in a bowl. Knowing that it was Dad's birthday coming up, she sorted through them until she found an old penny bearing the date 1919, the year of his birth, which she bought and presented to him as a gift. I still have that coin, which holds a special memory for me. Not just a memory of my father, but also of that generous, loving act of the nurse who cared far beyond that which was expected of her.

On the night of the 17th March, 1994, knowing that Dad's time on earth was drawing to a close, Graham and I sat with him, listening to his breathing and talking with him, trying to offer him strength and comfort. I can see him now, as he lay there pointing up at the ceiling and counting and saying something about lights. Whether it was the lights in the ward that he was counting, or whether he was seeing something that we could not see, I don't know. He told me that he was scared and I tried to help him by saying that there was nothing to worry about, that soon he would be with Mum again. He gave a weak smile and said *"And with Glenys"* the daughter they had lost so many years before. From that moment he settled into a peaceful rest; his breathing became weaker and in the early hours of 18th March 1994, he let go of his earthly life.

We often think of death as being something we have no control over, it is something that happens *to* us. From witnessing the deaths of both my parents, and from other experiences since then, I believe that we can have some control over when we choose to let go. I believe that my mother waited until I was there before she went, and I also believe that my father wanted to join his love, but waited until he had fulfilled his wish to celebrate his 75th birthday. Death is not some horrible thing that takes us when it wants to, but is just part of life and nothing to be feared.

As I trace the karmic line that connects all things in my life, I can see that had my parents not been diagnosed with cancer and had they not died in the way they did at Cransley Hospice in Kettering, then I would not be doing the work that I am now involved with, and *The Centre* in Swansea, of which you will read about later, would not have come into existence.

*

My relationship with my own two daughters has been markedly different to my parents' relationship with me. For a start, they didn't grow up with me being in their home, as their mother and I divorced when they were both very young. There are obviously lots of things and experiences we didn't share together in the same way that we would have done had we been together, but there are also lots of things that we have experienced that we may not have if we had shared the same home. I've got no intention of embarrassing them here with stories of their childhood, or even their adulthood. I think it is enough just to say that both Donna and Rhian have grown up into beautiful young women, both inwardly and outwardly. They have made their own decisions and choices in life and are both following their own paths, and very successfully so. I love them very much and have nothing but pride and respect for who they are and what they are doing with their lives.

Working Life

When I was very young, and people would ask, "*What do you want to be when you grow up?*" I would normally reply, "*a tester in a mattress factory*", such was my relationship with my bed and my love of sleep.

*

I grew up in a period of time when people could expect to have a job for life, it was not unusual for workers to be presented with a gold-watch in recognition of being with the same company for 50 years. The majority of people left school at the age of 15, went to work and retired when they reached the age of 65. We were told to choose our employment carefully as we would likely be there for a very long time. Things changed very quickly though in the 1970s, more people were going into higher education, they became a lot more mobile and moved around the country with greater ease, and it also became easier to emigrate to other lands. Technology and mechanisation made jobs less secure, as a piece of machinery was able to the same job that it would take a lot more individual workers to do. For me, the thought of being in the same job for 50 years, whatever it was, was not at all attractive. Thankfully, it was not to be something that I would have to endure.

I don't know who it was that originally said it, but a

phrase that has become one of those oft-repeated *"words-of-wisdom"* that is seen on postcards, posters and Facebook postings, yet holds so much truth, is about how *"we spend so much time trying to make a living, that we forget to make a life"*. During my working life I have had many jobs, some of them I have enjoyed, while others have been a strain and pure drudgery. At times I have worked solely for the money, whilst at other times it has been out of passion or desire. In the case of the latter there have been times when it has rewarded me with good money, and times when the reward has come in deeper, more lasting ways. The days when I feel I need to work to make a living have long gone, and I do what I do, simply because it feels right to do.

While I was still at school, most of the people I knew had paper-rounds which meant them getting up very early on 6 or sometimes 7 days a week, in all weathers, to deliver the morning papers, and then again after school with the evening paper. That was certainly not for me, I had cultivated a serious relationship with my bed and wasn't too keen to leave it in the mornings.

Together with my friend Tony, with whom I was at school throughout both our primary and secondary education, we managed to get jobs helping a local market trader on Fridays and Saturdays. On Friday we would go down to the open-air market in Kettering and help Dave, a market trader from London, unload his van and set up his stall before we set off to school. Dave's market stall sold men's trousers, jackets and jeans and at the end of the day we would make our way back to the market to help him break down the stall and load all the stock back into the van again.

On Saturdays we would do the same again and take it in turns to help sell things and look after the stall on alternate weekends. Tony would be there one week, and I would be there the following week. From there, I graduated to working in a men's fashion boutique every day after school for an hour or so and also all day on Saturday. During school holidays I would work full-time in the shop, *S. Lee & Sons* at Number One, the High Street. Howard Lee, who ran the Kettering shop for his mother, was a short, round, Jewish man in his early 30s who smoked Dunhill International cigarettes, a brand that I was later to favour when I indulged in the habit myself for a few years later on in my life. I continued working there throughout my time as a student at Kettering Technical College, right up until I started my first full-time job.

Each week when I was working in the shop, I would make a regular visit to Alf Bailey's, the local musical instrument and record shop, on a Saturday morning and hand over ten shillings from my wages as payment on account for the first guitar that I was to buy for myself, and which had been put away in the storeroom until I had paid the total price in full.

Working in the little boutique also had the added benefit to me of getting to see all the new fashions when they came into the shop and being able to get hold of the latest design in flared hipsters or kipper ties before anyone else did.

Because my parents had said an emphatic "no!" to me

going to drama school, the time came when I needed to get a proper job. I chose to follow one of my other passions, that of books, and got a job as a Library Assistant at Kettering Public Library. It wasn't my dream job, but it did turn out to be a lot less stuffy than I thought it might be. Mr Burden and Miss Haworth, who were the Head-Librarian and Deputy Librarian respectively, were pretty much what you would expect in such an institution, but I got on well with quite a few of the other, younger staff. Stephen Atterbury and Daphne Hewitt became good friends during my time there as we shared similar interests in life. Stephen and I were often given the job of looking after the record library, which housed a wonderful collection of mainly classical and jazz recordings, all on the hallowed vinyl. On the days when I got to sit in the record library, discovering and listening to recordings that were totally new to me, my taste in music developed and widened and I began to find enjoyment in sounds that had never held any interest for me before. I would thoroughly enjoy listening to classical orchestral pieces, choral works and the occasional jazz recording.

1971 arrived and I left home and moved to the land of my fathers, South Wales. I arrived in Swansea without a job, but in 1971 that was no problem as unemployment then was not a big cause for concern. There was lots of work in the area at that time with new industries springing up, together with the recently opened Driver & Vehicle Licensing Centre, bringing with it hundreds of new jobs. First stop on the morning after I arrived in Wales was an interview at the employment exchange. I had initially thought that I may get a job at the city library, but unfortunately there were no vacancies there, so I was sent for an interview with the *Trustees Savings Bank* and was straight away given a job as a bank-clerk. The first thing I had to do was to visit *Jackson's the Tailors* on the High Street and spend £20 on the purchase of a new suit in keeping with my new position at the bank.

It didn't take too long before I discovered that working in a bank was something that I most definitely did not want to be doing for the rest of my life. This was one of those situations that I mentioned earlier, where I was *"making a living"* rather than *"having a life"*. Once again, the staff that I found myself working with were great, really nice people; the job, however, for me was mindless. During the time I was working there, Britain went through the process of changing its currency system from pounds, shillings and pence, to the new decimal coinage. The bank had not yet installed computers in 1971, and all the accounts were hand-written in ledgers kept on shelves behind the main counter. Whenever anyone made a deposit, or a withdrawal, it had to be entered by hand into the ledgers. Decimalisation meant that one of my jobs in February 1971 was to go through all the accounts and convert the balance from £.s.d. into the new system of £.p.

On one occasion, when the bank was preparing to link into a national computerized system during the summer of 1971, the staff from our branch were taken to Shrewsbury to visit the central computer hub to be shown how the system would work. Things were so much different then, we were shown large rooms that were full of big cabinets that reached the ceiling, with reels of tape turning as the computers whirred and buzzed. I expect that 45 years later the equivalent of all that computer hardware would now fit into a briefcase, if not something smaller.

It soon became clear that I was just not interested in banking, and the thought of continuing in that type of work for any length of time was soul-destroying. Seeing the amount of money that some people were storing up in their accounts, alongside the lack of money in others, had a profound effect on me. Not only was I not interested in the work, I was most certainly not interested in being part of this system. I wanted to be doing something with my life, not just earning money and adding to the economy. I wanted to be doing something for other people, not just for myself.

After 9 months of working in the bank I had had enough and I handed in my notice. I started making enquiries with regards to doing some kind of volunteer or social work. A couple of friends I knew had given up a year of their time before going to university, in order to work with an organisation called Voluntary Service Overseas (VSO). As an organisation they would send volunteers to developing countries to assist in various projects to help the locals. I didn't feel that I was ready to travel overseas, but I discovered that VSO had a sister organisation; Community Service Volunteers (CSV), doing similar work, but here in the UK. I contacted them and was duly accepted as a volunteer. At the time, volunteers with CSV were paid an allowance of £2.50 a week and given board and lodgings wherever they were working.

During my time working with Community Service Volunteers I had two postings, one in Nantwich in Cheshire, at St Joseph's, a Roman Catholic run Approved School, what today would be known as a Secure Children's Home or Young Offenders Institute. My role there was to work as a liaison between the young offenders and the monks, who were members of the Brothers of Christian Schools, (or De La Salle Brothers) who ran the place and taught the boys. The system was awful and focused more on punishment than rehabilitation. Many of the boys were already totally institutionalised and deeply entrenched in the cycle of offending, getting caught, being punished, being released and offending again. The worst part was that alongside these already hardened offenders, were young boys who had done nothing wrong, other than the fact that they had come from broken homes and had absconded from the children's homes that they had been placed in. Such children were considered to be uncontrollable and as such were locked away in a place where they would likely learn, from the other inmates, how to become real criminals.

I don't know how much of a positive effect I had at St Joseph's as the monks there were so rigid and set in their ways that I felt that I wasn't really able to do the job that CSV had sent me there for. I don't know what it is like these days in Young Offenders Institutes, one would hope that they are a lot better than they were in the 1970s. Thankfully, St Joseph's Approved School has long gone, and hopefully some of the boys there were able to move on and lead healthy, happy lives.

My next position with CSV was far more useful and rewarding in so many ways. Venture House, in Woking, Surrey, was a children's home run by the charity, Ockenden Venture. Ockenden Venture had originally been set up by Joyce Pearce in 1951. The initial object of the charity was to receive small numbers of Eastern European teenagers from post World War II displaced persons camps in Germany, and to support them through their secondary education. Although the charity remained small in scale and personal in ethos, within a few years, world events and the increasing numbers of refugees worldwide, led it to widen both its remit and its scope; first to help children and students outside Europe during the 1960s, then to play a leading role in the admission and resettlement of Tibetans fleeing oppression, and the Vietnamese Boat People. Child victims of the conflict in Vietnam were brought to the UK in order to help them start a new life away from the horrors of war. It was with a great sense of pride many years later that I saw Joyce being honoured on the television programme, *This Is Your Life.*

The project that I was involved in at Venture House, was to provide a home for the children of Commonwealth students who were studying in Britain, but were unable to have their children with them for various reasons. There were 12 children living on Constitution Hill in Venture House, being looked after by 4 volunteers, myself, Hans, a German who had chosen volunteering work over serving in the armed forces for his National Service, and two girls, Anthea, from the Channel Islands and Ruth whose home was in Watford. We all lived on the premises and, in addition to the four of us, Mrs Melka, a lovely Estonian refugee was the main housekeeper and cook and her assistant Mira, another refugee from Yugoslavia, together with her young son, Mecho.

The children ranged in age from 15 months to 4 years old, and we also had two Vietnamese refugees living in the house. One a girl of about 19 years old and a young boy of about 8, called Nyang who, due to some horrific event in Vietnam had lost his ability to speak.

At last I felt I was actually doing something positive with my life. It didn't matter about the money; the reward was worth so much more than that. Things were so much different then, not one of us working at Venture House had undergone any training in child-care or social work, I don't think that there was anything that resembled CRB checks back then but certainly none of us had gone through any vetting process of any kind. We were just a group of young people who cared and wanted to make a difference. It was during my time with Ockenden Venture that I had my first contact with Tibetan Buddhist monks.

At the time, Constitution Hill was in a lovely leafy area of 1970s middle-class England, and a children's home full of beautiful black-skinned toddlers didn't sit well with many of the residents. Venture House had to close and it was with some sadness that the time came for me to move on again.

*

Some time before starting work as a Community

Service Volunteer, I had decided that I wanted to train to work with the Salvation Army and to become a Salvation Army officer. I began my training with them by undertaking a correspondence course that had to be completed in preparation for entering their Denmark Hill College in London. I was half-way through the course when Venture House closed down, and I was asked if I would be interested in looking after the Salvation Army centre in Resolven, a little Welsh village near the town of Neath. I was installed as the Commanding Officer in Resolven, with the rank of Envoy, under the experienced eye of Captain David Wilson who was the officer in charge of the nearby Salvation Army in Skewen. This began a new phase in my life where my main focus would be on the spiritual care of others.

Life was very different for me during the time I was with the Salvation Army, and my subsequent work, which I will talk about in a later chapter, as an evangelical preacher back in Swansea. It was all part of what I believed back then, although today I see that belief as being a very narrow form of spirituality which was extremely exclusive and far from liberating.

After leaving Resolven and returning to Swansea, I was given accommodation at the Bible College of Wales in exchange for work done with the boarders at the College's Emmanuel Grammar School, along with helping to keep the place clean. The boarders there were all children of missionaries who chose to leave their children in the care of others while they were preaching the gospel in other lands. For some of the children it was hard to understand why their parents seemed to be more concerned with others than they were with their own families. Others were told, and believed, that their parents were just following God's example when he sacrificed his only son for the sake of the world. I can't imagine how hard that must have been for the children.

I enjoyed my time working at the school and built up a good relationship with the pupils there. The experience of not being paid any money at all, but learning to trust that all my needs would be met, was both exciting and scary. Lessons were learnt that would stay with me throughout my life, until this present day.

I write more about my life-long spiritual journey in another part of this book so, for now, I will move on to the next steps in my working life.

*

My first wife, Carole, and I, met as a result of our shared faith, both attending the local church. It wasn't long before we were engaged and we discussed the financial implications of such an arrangement. It was felt that I needed to have a more secure income coming in if we were to get married and settle down. Gradually, I found myself slipping back into the *"working-for-a-living"* mode. First of all taking a part-time job as a warehouse man for the retail chemists, *Boots*, and then a job with a removal-firm. The removals work didn't last too long before I took a full-time job with the Post Office as a Postman. Getting up at 5 o'clock every day to deliver the mail came with mixed blessings; in the winter months it was possible to wrap up in multiple layers of warm clothing, and the freshness of the morning air was invigorating. Walking my beat every day also gave time for thinking and could be used as a perfect opportunity for contemplation. It wasn't so much fun when the rain was coming down and I would end up getting a thorough drenching. I do, however, particularly remember the summer of 1976, when the UK experienced a long spell of very hot and sunny weather. Every day, after having delivered the mail I would go back home for a change of clothes and then catch a bus to my favourite beach on the Gower with a good book and a sandwich, and spend the day relaxing on the rocks and dipping into the sea to cool down from time to time. It's forty years ago now, but I can still remember the wonderful feeling of freedom during that glorious summer.

After a few years of early morning walking, I was given the opportunity to apply for a job working behind the counter in the Post Office. Following an interview and a practical test, I was given the job, and I stayed there until after my first daughter, Donna, was born. Feeling more and more frustrated and hemmed in by the situation that I saw myself in, I started to look around for something else. As one of my gifts in life seems to be my ability to communicate, somebody suggested that I try for a job in sales and so I left the Post Office and took a job selling life assurance. It didn't take me long to realise that this was definitely not for me. Blinded by the prospect of being able to earn big money, I hadn't reckoned on my conscience and my reluctance to talk somebody into buying something that they really couldn't afford or didn't actually need. So after 4 months I took another sales job, which involved visiting shops to point out to the proprietors that they really needed to update their shop-fittings, and go for anything between a new counter and a complete refurbishment of the premises. A job, I have to admit, that I was totally useless at and which brought me to the acceptance that I was just not cut out for a job in sales.

The Post Office were good enough to take me back, but I was really not happy back in the situation of just having a job in order to make a living. What I really wanted to do was follow my life-long love of music and become a professional musician. I was faced with the pressure that was being put on me from all sides, reminding me that my priority now, with a second baby on the way, was to provide for my family and, to consider doing something because it was what I wanted to do, or that I had a passion for, was deemed to be selfish.

Things didn't get any better, my marriage broke up and I moved out of the family home. I continued working at the Post Office for some time before finally calling it a day. I had had enough of working for other people and organisations; it was time to start working for myself and to become officially self-employed. When I left the Post Office for the last time in 1983, I would never again have a *proper* job, I would never again have that security of knowing that at the end of the month there would be a salary paid into my bank account, I would never again have somebody else directing my life and trying to mould me into what I was not.

There would still be times that followed when I would

make mistakes, there would still be times when I would try to be what I thought was wanted of me, there would still be times when I would stumble and fall, and there would be lots of times when I would get up again and continue walking, but it would always be my choice, my decision.

*

My first venture into a life of being self-employed was to venture into the retail world by opening my first business, *Body & Soul*. *Body & Soul* was a small unit in a Swansea shopping-centre selling a range of items from hand-made body-lotions and shampoos to esoteric books - just what it said above the door, a place where you could care for both your body and your soul. As well as selling through the shop, I also went on the road to exhibit and trade at New Age shows around the country, travelling to places like Manchester, London, Bristol, and Nottingham. Doing these shows on a regular basis was like being part of a travelling community of like-minded people who became great friends along the way. I also ventured into organising a few of these New Age events in Swansea and started publishing and editing *Unicorn Magazine*, a quarterly publication devoted to New Age Spirituality. Running the shop and travelling up and down the country meant that the business was not a massive financial success, to say the least, but it was fun and I was able to take my guitar out of its case when needed, go out onto the streets and spend a couple of hours busking in order to supplement my income.

As it turned out, the busking proved to be a lot more enjoyable and lucrative, and certainly less stressful, than running the shop. Rather than trying to balance the books with the business, I opted for a life of playing music. The freedom of getting up each day and heading into town, or getting on a bus or train to head for new places, and spending a couple of hours brightening up the day for passers-by until I had earned enough to meet my basic, simple needs, was fantastic. I loved the experience of meeting people and seeing their appreciation, who knows how many days were brightened for people as they walked by?

During the years of playing my music on the streets of Swansea, Worcester, Malvern and a few other places I also started getting paid bookings in folk-clubs and pubs. It was also at this time that I met, and married my second wife, Andrea. Together we also started a small craft business and specialised in decorating wooden items, using pyrography. Using a tool, very similar to a soldering iron, but with pen-like nibs, we would burn Celtic knot-work designs on various decorative and practical items. The travelling continued as we exhibited at craft fairs up and down the country at weekends, while I continued to play my music on the streets during the week.

One of the organisations that we worked with, Four Seasons Events, used to put on themed, costumed, craft-fairs in England and, hearing that I was a musician, they booked me to be one of their regular entertainers, which was a welcome, regular income during the summer months. I was also starting to pick up more and more bookings to play music in various venues and, as this increased, I was able to give up the busking and concentrate on building a career as a musician. Festival bookings were also coming in, and I played my first Glastonbury festival in the early 1980s which led to an association that has continued right up until now. I now hold the position of Area Organiser for The John Peel Stage, one of the four main stages, at what has been voted the world's best international music festival, for 9 years running, by the Pollstar Concert Industry Awards ceremony in Nashville, Texas.

Pretty soon I found myself working at venues around the country for 6 or 7 nights a week, along with my musical partner, Ian "Tich" Thomas and also various bands that I played with. We found ourselves spending much time driving up and down the British motorways, often having to be nudged awake at the wheel while driving home from a gig at 3 o'clock in the morning. Over the years, my performances have taken me to many countries, including Ireland, France, Norway and Denmark. Denmark became something of a second home to me as I spent around 4 or 5 months a year touring this beautiful country and getting to make many friends during my time there.

Somewhere in the middle of all this my marriage to Andrea came to an end and we decided to go our separate ways. I continued for a while with the craft business until my musical career took total precedence. Songs were written, CDs were recorded, festivals, theatres, concert halls and bars were played and life was good. It was at one of my performances in 1999 that I spotted a very special lady in the audience, and Kiera and I were married in the spring of 2006.

During the 80s and 90s, alongside everything else that I was doing, I also got heavily involved with the theatre, which had been a passion of mine since schooldays. I was initially asked to help run a local village Youth Theatre in Pontardawe, near Swansea, and that led on to me being asked to work with the Swansea Grand Youth Theatre, based at the city's main theatre venue. In the years that followed I was involved in producing, directing and writing a number of productions that were performed at the theatre in Swansea, and at a number of other local venues.

On one occasion the Youth Theatre members wanted me to write a musical that they could perform. I had never attempted such a project before. I set about writing *Weavers*, which was a musical based on the legend of King Arthur, but focusing on the women in his life. The Swansea Youth Theatre production of *Weavers* went on to represent Swansea at the National Youth Theatre Festival where it was performed in Ilfracombe in Devon and we also took it out on a small, but really enjoyable tour, which was a great experience for the young members of the Youth Theatre.

When writing *Weavers,* I included a few songs that I had written previously, along with some brand new ones written specifically for the show. The basis of the script was quite easy as I had been familiar with various versions of the Arthurian legends for some time. A particularly favourite retelling of the legend was *Mists of Avalon,* written by Marion Bradley. The rest of the script was put together as a result of some improvisation workshops done with the Youth Theatre members, with the help of my assistant director, Mike Waters.

It has been wonderful in the years that have followed, to see so many of those Youth Theatre members go on and develop their own careers, and establish themselves in theatre, film and television. Some of them went on to pursue careers as actors, some as directors, some as teachers and others, like my own daughter, Donna, as stage-managers.

A couple of the songs that I included in *Weavers* became some of my most popular compositions, and I still include them in my occasional concerts today. One in particular, *Summerlands,* is a favourite of mine and is particularly fitting for the work that I find myself involved with today.

Summerlands

I never thought it was easy, but I know it's been worthwhile, walking this way.
I know I've had my problems
And questions in my mind
But I've lived, to face today.

And in the Summerlands,
When this life is over
And we've left this world of men
In the Summerlands,
When this life is over
I know the sun will shine again.

We walked this road together
You were priestess to my priest
We travelled the ancient way
And we danced the ring at the old stones
And we shared the cakes and wine
We made love at the dawning of the day.

We've stood within the circle
Many times before
In many different lives
But no matter what we came through,
Through water or through fire,
Love survives.

And in the Summerlands,
When this life is over
And we've left this world of men.
In the Summerlands,
When this life is over
I know the sun will shine again.

One thing that always struck me as a performing musician was how much of an effect different types of music could have on one's audience. Depending on what was played, an audience could be influenced to get up and dance, clap in time with a regular rhythm or sometimes they would be touched so deeply on an emotional level that they could be brought to tears. We have probably all experienced walking along the street and finding that our steps have synchronised with the beat of the music playing from inside the shops, or a brass band playing on the street.

When my daughter, Donna, bought me a Tibetan Singing Bowl as a birthday present one year, I was amazed at the instant sense of peace and calm that it brought to me when I played it. This was a power that I hadn't experienced before from any type of music and I had to find out more. I started to read whatever information I could find about the singing bowls and how they worked, and became absorbed by the amazing energy that they seemed to hold and transmit. One of the first books I read was by Mitchell L Gaynor, an American oncologist. His book, *The Healing Power of Sound, Recovery from life-threatening illness using Sound, Voice and Music,* related stories of how he used the sound of these bowls when treating cancer patients in his clinic, and the remarkable results that he was seeing. It was that book in particular that helped me to make my decision to train as a Sound Therapist.

I enrolled on a course taught by Leslie Carol at Atlantis College in Somerset, and began my training, learning all about the healing vibration of sound and the different instruments that could be used, including the

Tibetan bowls, Crystal Singing Bowls, Tribal Drums and the wonderful energy of Gongs. This was an incredibly exciting time in my life and Sound Therapy continues to play a major role in my work as a qualified practitioner and teacher. Working with clients as they come to me with their various problems has enabled me to witness some amazing results as people have experienced pain-relief along with the healing benefits of sound vibrations. Likewise, the privilege of being able to teach others how to use sound in a therapeutic and healing way is something that one cannot put a price on.

I had my own encounter with the power of sound, with what some may call a *'miraculous'* healing, not long after I began my practitioner therapy training. Around 2003 I was on holiday in the South of France when I was suddenly hit with a tremendous pain, the like of which I had never previously experienced. All down my left arm was in agony, and my fingertips on my left hand had lost all sensation. My initial thought was that I was having a heart attack. Kiera, who at the time was a student nurse, checked me out and confidently ruled-out that possibility. The pain was so intense that we had to cut the holiday short and return home. Before flying back to Britain, I saw a French doctor at the airport in Nice, who gave me a strong pain-killing injection, which, although making sitting down rather uncomfortable, eased the pain for the length of the journey. Unfortunately the relief was short lived and the pain returned and for some time I was unable to find comfort in any position.

When I got back home to Wales, my own GP prescribed

painkillers and anti-inflammatory medication but was unable to diagnose the problem. He also suggested a course of acupuncture treatment and physiotherapy. The physiotherapy did nothing to help the situation. The acupuncture did have some success in relieving the pain but failed to get to the root of the problem. I was eventually referred for an MRI scan at the local hospital and, after waiting several months, was diagnosed with Osteoarthritis. The scan revealed that I had a piece of bone growing from my spine towards the spinal column, which was touching on the nerve pathway that travelled between my left arm and my brain. This was a diagnosis that revealed that I was suffering from exactly the same condition that had caused my father such discomfort and problems, details of which I have outlined in an earlier chapter.

The consultant neurosurgeon was very eager to get his knives out and to operate on me at the earliest opportunity, informing me that a sudden braking in the car, or a slip on an icy pavement, could result in me being permanently paralysed from the neck down, information that he emphasised with a creepy smile and a flat-hand gesture slicing across his throat. I wasn't sure that I wanted to give my consent without knowing all the pros and cons of what the operation involved, so, with the help of my wife, decided to do my own research first. The operation would involve an incision at the front of my neck, moving my vocal chords out of the way to allow the surgeon to chisel away the offending bone-growth before repairing the damaged bone. Success couldn't be guaranteed and there would also be the danger of various side-effects such as resulting in incontinence, loss of, or damage to, the voice, or even permanently damaging the spinal cord causing the very paralysis that the operation was trying to avoid.

Taking everything on balance, I decided not to go ahead with the operation. I was not going to worry about what might happen, but rather try to live in the moment and face any problems if and when they arose. The pain I was experiencing now seemed to be under control, although the most that I could feel in my fingertips was a constant numbness.

It was around this time that I was embarking on my training as a Sound Therapist & Healer and I began to notice that, after a weekend of intensive use of the singing bowls and the healing energy of the voice, my symptoms were improving and my fingers were beginning to "feel" again. Over the course of the next few months, all pain disappeared and the sensation in my fingers returned to normal. I cannot prove that it was working with sound-vibrations that brought about this healing, but I certainly believe that it was. To this day, everything is working normally and, although I have not had another MRI scan to confirm what I believe, I am convinced that the bone-growth that was causing the problem has now gone and that my spine is just the way that it is meant to be. Just as when an opera singer hits a certain vocal frequency, which can smash a glass into tiny pieces, it has been shown that sonic frequencies can cause such things as gall-stones or kidney-stones to disintegrate. This is what I believe happened to the bone protruding from my spine.

Personally, I don't believe that this sort of healing is

miraculous, but rather that it should be something that we can all experience at any time that we need it, when we come to understand that healing and well-being is something natural, not supernatural, and normal, not miraculous.

*

Around about this time, Kiera and I started a new venture with *Labyrinth Magazine*. Together we edited and published the magazine, which focused on holistic life-style, covering such subjects as complementary medicine, holistic spirituality, nutrition etc. We ran everything from our home, which often meant that one side of the staircase would be full of boxes of magazines waiting to be delivered. We also handled all the distribution ourselves, travelling around South and West Wales visiting shops, health-centres, community halls and various other places where people could pick up their free copy. We were honoured to have articles offered from a wide range of contributors including a Tibetan Lama, a Benedictine Monk, a Hay House author and many others. Due to the cost of producing *Labyrinth* we eventually decided to make it an online publication, but when other demands started to take priority, we sadly had to call it a day.

*

Kiera had now qualified as a nurse and was particularly drawn to working with people as they approached the end of their lives. Because of my own experience with the deaths of both my parents, I too felt some sort of calling to work in the same area. As we shared our thoughts together we felt that what we wanted was to be able to provide some sort of holistic centre where we could offer support, together with free complementary therapy treatments, to those living with cancer and other types of life-limiting conditions. We felt it was also important to be able to offer this support and treatment to their carers as well. So often, those who care for the sick are forgotten and neglected at a time when what they themselves are going through can be just as traumatic and frightening. We also felt drawn to the idea of opening a hospice but we had no idea how we could possibly achieve any of this vision, as at the time we had no money and no real prospects of being able to raise the capital to turn the idea into a reality.

We had organised a Healing Camp in West Wales, where we had gathered together a number of healers and practitioners, who were offering their services and leading workshops throughout the weekend. The centrepiece of the camp was a beautiful Cretan labyrinth, which was open for people to use for meditation throughout the weekend. One of the purposes of a labyrinth meditation is that you can enter the labyrinth with a particular question or dilemma as your focus and by the time you either reach the centre, or leave the labyrinth, you are ready to receive the wisdom that will enable you to act.

Kiera and I entered the labyrinth together, knowing that we both shared this vision without knowing how to accomplish, or manifest it. As soon as I made my first step onto the path, I knew. It was clear and simple, just like a light being switched on in my soul. A labyrinth is not to be confused with a maze. When you walk through a maze you are confronted with turnings, which may lead you to a dead-end, causing frustration and a lot of wasted time. When you walk a labyrinth however, there is only one path. At times it may seem that the path is taking you round in circles and further away from your destination, but that one path will always lead you to the centre. At that moment I knew that in order to reach the place that was our goal, our purpose, if you like, all that had to be done was to keep walking. By taking one step at a time, following the path and keeping moving, the destination would be reached. Yes, there would be times when it would feel like one was moving further away, or going round in circles without making any progress, but I knew that by keeping going and moving forwards, then one could not fail to reach the centre, the destination. It was time to stop worrying about how we could make it happen, time to stop stressing and concentrating on the problems, and time to start trusting and focusing on the journey, rather than the destination. I was reminded of a well-known verse from the ancient Chinese writings, the Tao Te Ching, which says, *"A journey of a thousand miles begins with a single step"*

At that time, I was renting a therapy room above an holistic shop where I was practicing Sound Therapy. Unfortunately the shop wasn't doing too well and the owner took the decision to close the business, which meant I was going to be without a therapy room. The date for closure was set as 28th February 2011. Two weeks before the shop was due to close, I received a phone call saying that I had been chosen to appear on a television game show, and I would need to be available for 3 weeks beginning on March 1st, in order to start recording. The timing was perfect, it was to be the day after the shop was closing, and it looked like things were beginning to move forwards. This was an opportunity to come home with some money to enable us to start taking steps towards our dream.

The show was *"Deal or No Deal"* and when the time came to play my game, Kiera and I were able to talk on air about our vision of the holistic centre and our desire to work with those living with life-limiting conditions. Our words were to be broadcast to around 2 million people across the UK. We walked away from the show with a cheque for £15,000, which was the start of something that was to continue to grow over the coming months.

When the show was aired in the following November, one particular viewer was reminded of a similar vision that she had had many years before, but for one reason or another she had never been able to see it come to fruition. She felt that she wanted to help, but at the time had no spare money to offer. We received a letter from Elsie the following March in which she told us that on March 1st, exactly one year after I walked into the television studio, she had won a substantial sum on the monthly UK Premium Bond draw and subsequently sent us a cheque for £20,000. Although we have spoken on the telephone, and exchanged letters since that time, I have never actually had the pleasure of meeting Elsie, but both Kiera and I will always be grateful for her amazingly generous gift.

During that year, and following my "light-bulb moment" in the labyrinth, we received over £65,000 from various, and unexpected, sources. Even today, more than 5 years later, we are still finding that the Universe is providing for us in unexpected ways and enabling us to continue the work that we were able to start. Just recently I received a cheque from my bank for several hundred pounds as a repayment for charges that they had wrongly made which related to my time working in Denmark, and the transfers of money from Denmark to the UK. Even without having to ask, the Universe finds a way of providing. That was just one of many instances when money came to us in unexpected ways.

In order to open our holistic centre, we first needed to find some suitable premises and, just as before, it seemed like we weren't getting anywhere. The places were either too big or too small, or in need of too much work. Once again we had to go back to the lesson of the Labyrinth and make the decision to stop trying to force it, as this was only causing us to get stressed with the frustration of hitting brick walls, and instead just to wait until the right place revealed itself to us.

Soon afterwards, it happened! I was paying a visit to the bank and had parked in a car park that I had used on many previous occasions. This time though, I happened to notice a sign in a building opposite saying "*office space to rent*". Thinking that this might give us somewhere to practise our therapies whilst we continued to look for something more permanent, I called in to make enquiries. It immediately felt right; the current occupier was planning on downsizing and was looking at renting out two or three rooms on the first floor. After talking to him and explaining our vision for what we wanted to do, the offer of two or three rooms turned into the whole building and he offered to re-locate his whole business so that we could take over the entire premises. I had simply been in the right place at the right time.

Within four weeks we moved in to what is now The Centre and so began the next stage of my working life. From The Centre we are able to offer the services of support and therapy treatments that we had set out to provide. What is more, we have been able to do so without having to charge those who were living with such life-limiting conditions as cancer, Motor Neurone Disease etc., as well as offering the same support to their carers.

However, the road to being able to fulfil the original vision of opening an actual hospice was to take a totally different route from the one we had anticipated.

Initially, it was through Kiera's nursing work that we were introduced to the community at Skanda Vale, in West Wales. The community members there had already been running a day hospice service, which Kiera had been able to visit during her nursing training, and they had embarked on a project to raise money to renovate their building and turn it into a residential hospice, catering for six in-patients. Work was completed in early 2016 and Kiera is now working with the community as a senior nurse and deputy manager at Skanda Vale Hospice and I am able to offer my own services from time to time as a Sound Therapist.

As our work with those facing their final days developed, we became more aware of how the subject of death and dying was something that was so often swept under the carpet. It seemed that people didn't want to talk about it, particularly the families of those who were actually dying. We had heard about such things as *Death Cafés* where people could discuss end of life matters in a safe and supported environment, and also the *Kicking The Bucket Festival* which takes place in Oxford and is organized by Liz Rothschild; and we decided that it would be a good idea to organise something similar in Swansea.

The first *Elephant In The Room* event took place in Swansea in October 2014, a four-day event that included a full programme of talks and workshops. Subjects covered included end of life care, bereavement counselling, legal aspects such as will-writing and advance decisions, funeral planning etc. The weekend also featured Antonia Rolls' wonderful art-exhibition called *A Graceful Death,* a production of Laura Wade's play *Colder Than Here* and a musical concert. The event proved to be an incredible success and requests started to come in for us to take it to other areas. So far we have organised *Elephant In The Room* events in Dorchester and at Skanda Vale Hospice, with further events planned in various places in the future. It has become a real passion of ours to encourage people to talk about a subject that none of us can avoid in the end.

*

In hindsight it is now easy to see that all the different

jobs and careers that have been part of my life, have been linked together by that thread of Karma, one after the other, bringing me to where I am now. All these things have brought me to the place where I am able to share my journey through my writing and through teaching. All I have had to do is to keep moving, to keep following the path of the labyrinth, one step leading to another, cause followed by effect.

Today I am writing this, my third book, next week I may be at The Centre, looking after the running of things there, on another day I may be leading a meditation or Kirtan group, on yet another I will be teaching Sound Therapy or giving a treatment to someone who needs it. These are the things that I do, they are not who I am.

As you can see, amongst other things during my working life, I have been a librarian, a retail worker, a carer, a bank clerk, a warehouse man, a removal man, a postman, a salesman, a craft-worker, a musician, a therapist, a teacher and a writer, but I am none of these things. These are just labels that have been put on me, things that I do or have done, they are not who I am.

It is all too easy to look at someone and only see them as the role they play, rather than to recognise that they are so much more than that. To recognise as well that what they do one day may be totally different to what they might do on another day. When we define someone by what they do, what happens when they stop doing that? Do they lose their identity? Do they cease to "be"? A person is not what he or she "does".

When we look closer and look deeper, we see beyond the office-worker or the street-cleaner, the scientist or the shop assistant, and we see the soul, the real identity of the one we encounter. We see the true value of the person.

Musical Life

Music has always played a massive part in my life and has been a major influence along my journey. The experiences that I have had as a result of my life in music, and the people that I have met along the way, have all played a contribution in bringing me to where I am today. My Mother wasn't particularly musical and didn't show any outward flare for either playing an instrument or for singing, but my father had an impressive baritone voice and, as a member of The Salvation Army, often took to the stage to sing. One of his favourite songs to perform was the old hymn, *Bless This House* that had been made famous by another Swansea boy, the comedian and entertainer, Harry Secombe.

Even though I grew up with music all around me, it took a long time for me to find out where it fitted in to my life, or perhaps more importantly, where I fitted in to the musical life. At school I learned to play the recorder, as did just about every other child at that time. The staple tunes of *Frère Jacques*, *Pease Pudding Hot* and *Three Blind Mice* are indelibly engraved on my mind. I sang in the choir, both at school and in The Salvation Army, where I had to attend regularly as a child. At the age of 7 it was expected, and required, that one would learn to play an instrument in preparation to join the band. Weeknight practices with the band, plus an additional personal tuition didn't seem to have much effect however. I started off on the cornet, moved to the tenor-horn, followed by the baritone and E flat bass. Unfortunately for my teachers I didn't actually excel at any of these brass instruments. Eventually they gave me a set of sticks and put me behind the big bass drum. Again, this did not prove to be fruitful. I remember on one occasion continuing to beat out the pounding rhythm on the drum when the rest of the band had already come to the end of the particular piece of music that we were playing.

For as long as I can remember, the only instrument that I really wanted to play was the guitar. I listened to the pop-songs of the day, people like Tommy Steele and Cliff Richard & The Shadows and that was what I wanted, I wanted to play the guitar and to sing like them. My dream was to own a Burns electric guitar, like the one that Hank Marvin played. I even remember entering a competition on the back of a *Cornflakes* packet to try and win one of these beautiful black guitars.

I was probably about 7 years old when my Uncle Ivor bought me a toy guitar. I can just about see it now in my memory, more like a ukulele than a guitar, brown in colour with nylon strings. I loved that guitar even though I had no idea how to tune it, let alone play it.

It was my brother, Graham, who got the first real guitar in our house. I can still remember one particular tune that he learnt to play on it as he practised for hours. The tune was *La Mer*, written by Charles

Tennet, but that was about as far as he was to get with it at the time. I inherited the guitar from him when he decided that he was never going to become the next Anton Segovia. With that guitar, and a six-shilling copy of Bert Weedon's misleadingly titled book, *Play in a Day*, I threw myself into learning how to master the art of guitar playing. I was determined to ride through the pain of the steel strings cutting in to my fingertips, as I would practise every day playing tunes like *"Frankie and Johnny"* and *"Jingle Bells"*.

Throughout my life, music has been a way for me to express myself. It has been a way to release myself from pain, from emotional stress, a way to free myself from the bonds and restrictions of life, and a way to celebrate joy in my life. I can remember that even at the early age of 12 or 13 I would sit in my bedroom with the guitar and write words to go with the four chords, G, Em, C & D, that I had just about got to grips with, trying to express what I was feeling inside.

I mentioned in a previous chapter that at the age of 15, I was working in a shop after school and on Saturdays, earning real money that I could spend on myself. After starting out on my brother's guitar, I eventually bought my own guitar, paying instalments each week out of my hard-earned wages. I can't remember exactly how much the guitar actually cost back then, but it did take quite a few weeks of paying the instalments before I was finally able to take it home with me. I quickly set about learning some folk songs and started to perform them at the Salvation Army youth club and at home for friends and anyone else who would listen. I had found my instrument; it was something that I felt comfortable playing and could relate to as an extension of my self.

That guitar, bought when I was just 15 years old, turned out to be the first of many such instruments that I would buy throughout my life and now, nearly 50 years later, I am still playing, and expressing myself through music, even though the music I mainly play today has a different feel and purpose to it than it did back then.

I am forever grateful for the opportunities that music has afforded me throughout my life. From busking in all weathers, sometimes going home with only a couple of pounds after four or five hours on the street, to performing a solo spot on one of the main stages at Glastonbury Festival, to playing accompaniment to the sacred songs, chants and Bhajans of Kirtan and Bhakti Yoga. It has been an incredible journey for which I give thanks.

I used to love the busking when I started out, people were generally appreciative of the fact that the music would cheer them up as they went about their daily routines of shopping and working. Busking didn't always provide a good living but I was determined that I would not resort to claiming government benefits when I could use my musical abilities to bring in what I needed. Christmas time was a different story altogether, with the help of a red suit and white beard, (this was at a time before my own beard had turned white) and a handful of up-beat Christmas songs, the takings would be very good indeed. I only knew about four or five seasonal songs, but one of the joys of busking is that people don't hang around for long periods of time, so you could repeat the songs as often as you liked.

Work started to come in from other places as pub landlords and music promoters got to see and hear me, and eventually I was able to call time on the busking and earn a living in the warm and dry. One of the biggest boosts came with the arrival of the now ubiquitous Irish bar. Every town and city boasted at least one O'Neill's, O'Donnell's, Waxy's, Flanagan's or some other variation of an Irish pub, and all of them wanted live Irish music. There just weren't enough Irish bands and musicians around to fill all the gigs, so, never one to miss an opportunity, I learnt a load of traditional and modern Irish songs and got together with various other musicians, and we hit the road with our own brand of blarney. With so many Irish bars popping up and so few Irish bands to play in them, the money we would be paid was far more than the usual fees for pub bands.

We had more work than we could physically cope with, and would be out on the road, the length and breadth of the UK, playing, sometimes 6 nights a week. I remember doing one stretch with my fellow guitarist, Tich, of 14 nights in a row without a break. I can't say that it was always good fun, but for 99% of it, it probably was. Tich and I would spend so much time driving up and down motorways as we travelled to gigs from Plymouth to Cleethorpes, Exeter to Newcastle and all stops in between. We got to know the good Bed and Breakfast establishments in each town, and also found quite a few that we vowed to avoid on our next visit. One memorable place, which was never to be visited again, was a very dodgy boarding house in Hove. It was the closest B & B we could find to Brighton that we could actually afford, and when we got there we soon found out why. It was more of a doss-house than a guest-house, inhabited by dubious characters and bearing some strange and unpleasant stains on the bedroom walls.

In 1983 I went along to enjoy my first Glastonbury Festival experience. Glastonbury Festival is the largest performing arts festival in Europe, attracting acts from all over the world. Back in 1983 it was a lot smaller than it has become today, but still the atmosphere was amazing. Apart from the iconic main stage, designed as a pyramid, there were a number of smaller and more intimate stages. On one of those less imposing stages I was introduced to some music that, although I didn't know it at the time, would come to play a big part in my future spiritual life. A band called *Court of Miracles*, who featured the wonderful voice of Jacki Whitten, were singing the mantra, *Om Namaha Shivaya*, sacred words that many years later I would be singing and recording myself.

My guitar went with me to Glastonbury and I managed to get myself a spot on one of the small acoustic stages in the Greenfields area of the festival. The stage was great with a really relaxed and informal atmosphere, the only thing missing, was somebody to introduce the performers, and so no one knew exactly who it was that they were watching. I had a chat with the organisers and offered my services as a compére, an offer that was welcomed with open arms. So began my long association with the best festival in the world. I was asked to come back the following year, not as a punter but as a bone-fide artist with my own Performers Ticket

After a couple of years working in the Greenfields, playing as a solo act and also with *The Fox Band* and *The Pig & Whistle Band* with my long time friend, Nigel Mason, I was eventually booked to perform my music on the Avalon Stage and also to share the duties of compére there with Phil Beer, from Show of Hands, and Graham Russell. A few years later the whole production team from the Field of Avalon was asked to take on the task of running a new area at the festival, called the New Bands Stage and I happily went with them. This was the start of a new, exciting period, firstly in my now familiar role introducing the acts and then, added to this, I was given the responsibility of Stage Manager, in charge of the two- dozen or so stage crew.

John Peel, the BBC Disc Jockey and presenter, was a regular visitor to the New Bands Stage as he presented the TV coverage from the festival each year. When he died in 2004, it was decided by Michael Eavis, the main organiser and founder of the Glastonbury Festival, that we should rename the stage as *'The John Peel Stage'*, in his honour. This was, and still is, a fitting tribute to a man who had an enormous influence on the British music scene. Six years later, in 2010, due to a reorganisation of the festival management, I was given the role of Area Organiser for the John Peel Stage. The couple of dozen people that I had been responsible for, now grew to a total crew of nearly 300. This fantastic crew look after everything

101

from drawing up the site plans, administration, catering, artist liaison teams, sound, light, video, press liaison, toilets, traffic management, massage therapies, stewards and anything else you could think of that was involved in the production of one of the four main stages at a festival that attracted nearly 180,000 ticket holders each year.

More than thirty three years after attending the festival for the first time as a paying member of the public, I am now being paid for a few months each year to do a job that I love, in a part of the UK that is very special and holds a deep spiritual history.

Over those thirty-odd years I have had the experience of working with and meeting some amazing people, and each one of them holds some special and significant memories. In 1999 I introduced a young band onto the New Bands Stage. Having just finished their final exams at University, they arrived with minutes to spare, having gone to the wrong end of the festival site, but *Coldplay* went on to become the massive act that they are today. That same year other acts to share the stage before they were famous, were *Muse*, *David Gray*, and *Dodgy*. Headlining that year was the legendary, *Patti Smith*. Other people that I have had the pleasure to introduce over the years for their first Glastonbury performances include *The Magic Numbers*, *The Killers*, *Mumford and Sons* and *George Ezra*.

2009 was the year that Michael Jackson died, and the news spread around the festival site with nobody knowing if it was just another Glastonbury rumour, or whether there was truth in it. It was also the year that

I had a message to say that Bruce Springsteen would be at the side of the stage to watch a young band from his home town in New Jersey, *The Gaslight Anthem*. The band invited him on stage to play with them, the word went round and the tent quickly filled up to witness Springsteen playing in a much smaller setting than is usual for him. After the show, Bruce and I talked for a while and I was genuinely impressed with the man and his interest in up and coming acts – definitely one of the highlights of my Glastonbury career.

The most surreal moment for me at Glastonbury came in 2013. I had received a message to say that Michael Eavis had some guests who wanted to come backstage at the John Peel Stage to have lunch, and could I arrange it. I naturally said yes and arranged for 20 or so guests to be fed in our catering tent. I wasn't told who the guests were, but as the request came from the man himself, I thought nothing of it. The guests arrived, led by one of the festival management team, and I took them all into the catering tent. They had turned up at exactly the time that I was to do an interview with Steve Lamaq, the BBC presenter, so I left the visiting party queuing up to get their meals at the counter.

I went off to do my interview, and when I returned about 30 minutes later, there were Michael's guests sitting at the tables, and for the first time I realised who I had left standing with a tray in his hands, queuing for his food. Prince Harry was probably the last person that I expected to see in a muddy field at a music festival, but there he was, together with a posse of other celebrities, and three or four bodyguards trying to look inconspicuous in spite of the very obvious bulges inside their t-shirts, concealing their firearms. I made my apologies for having to leave them earlier and Prince Harry was very understanding. He wanted to know how long I had been involved with the festival and showed his interest in all things "backstage", and the logistics of getting it all together. After a brief visit to the side of the stage to watch one of the bands, he then left us to go into the main part of the tent, along with all the other festival-goers in the mud.

I have encountered a lot of inflated egos over the years at Glastonbury, more often than not it is the acts who are just breaking through, they have perhaps just had their first taste of success with a hit recording and think that they are more important than they actually are. I have usually found that the bands who are further down the bill, and play earlier on in the day are great to work with, they are just grateful and excited about having the opportunity to play at Glastonbury. At the other end of the scale are the experienced ones who have got over all the ego stuff and just want to play their music and entertain their fans, again these are usually really easy to work with. It is often the ones in the middle who cause the problems and make the demands. Prince Harry was a great example of humility, he could have been just anybody, and that's probably what he wanted; no fussing, no fawning, just wanting to be allowed to be an ordinary person in a crowd of ordinary people. After he had finished his meal in the catering tent, he was the only one of his group who took the trouble to take his dirty plates back to the counter and to thank the staff for his lunch.

*

Meanwhile my own career as a performer was going from strength to strength. Tich and I, along with our fiddle player Kate Ronconi, were booked to do some shows in Norway and my love affair with Scandinavia began. The week in Norway was a real eye-opener in many ways. The respect with which musicians were treated was so different to how it was back home. With all our food and accommodation paid for it wasn't necessary to spend any of our own money apart from on a few extra luxuries or gifts that we wanted to buy. We were having a great time, living the rock-and-roll lifestyle, until our very last day in Bergen.

We had decided to go shopping for souvenirs before heading off to the airport, but unfortunately Tich had not quite got used to the fact that in Norway they drive on the right-hand side of the road as opposed to the left-hand side as here in Britain. As the three of us stood by the side of the pavement, waiting to cross, Tich stepped out having looked the wrong way. He hadn't seen the bus coming from the opposite direction and the bus-driver put his foot on the brake, stopping just as he made contact with Tich, who went flying through the air, landing with a thump on the road. With a couple of broken ribs and a punctured lung, he was not allowed to fly home with us and had to stay in hospital in Norway for another week or so until his injuries had started to heal. Kate and I flew back to Gatwick without him and he followed later, having spent time in a Norwegian hospital being carefully looked after by some young Scandinavian nurses, about which I don't recall him complaining. Other than that it was a wonderful week.

That was the first of my numerous visits to Scandinavia. Over a period of about 6 or 7 years I would spend around 4 months each year touring Denmark as a solo act with the occasional trip over to Norway. I love Scandinavia, particularly Denmark. The people, the pace of life, the atmosphere, just about everything that there is that makes up such a wonderful part of the world. The audiences at all the concerts were appreciative and welcoming, the hospitality was generous and the culture was warm, even if the climate wasn't always so.

The nineties and naughties were a particularly productive time for me with regard to song-writing. Sometimes the songs would be inspired by actual events and experiences, and sometimes totally fictitious. During this time I released a number of CDs, which featured original songs that I had written, some of which faded into obscurity while a few others became favourites of my audiences. It is a great feeling to stand in front of an appreciative crowd as they sing along to the words that one has written. Still today, whenever I get on stage I am asked to sing "*Summerlands*" and "*Time Goes On*", probably the two songs for which I am most proud. At the other end of the creative scale are songs like "*Glastonbury Mud*" and "*The Blue Skoda*", two songs that people always want me to sing, and two that I seldom want to sing. I did however recently sing "*The Blue Skoda*" at the funeral of a very dear friend, who was actually the inspiration for the song. Dennis was a very talented cartoonist who used to hire a car whenever he had to travel for his work. Often he would show up driving something quite flashy and expensive, but on one occasion he arrived in a Skoda that he had hired. This was at a time when the Skoda was not exactly the best built, or most reliable car and so I felt compelled to write a song at his expense. When he was coming to the end of his life he requested that I sing it at his funeral, and I was more than happy to oblige. Not exactly the 23rd Psalm, but it was what he wanted.

In 1998 I was asked to contribute some songs for an International Primary Schools teaching aid on the theme of Christmas. Three of my songs were published, one in the style of a traditional Christmas Carol, one about the joys of unwrapping presents on Christmas Day, and a third which was a sad song about a Snowman melting on Boxing Day. This last song contained some of the most groan-worthy rhymes ever to be included in a children's song.

The Snowman

It's not very long since I came into being,
But my eyes can't believe what they're really seeing.
You're probably wondering why I'm standing here whining,

You see I'm a poor snowman, and the sun has started shining.

(chorus)
Being a snowman isn't much fun,
When you wake up on Boxing Day to be greeted by the sun.
I can't begin to tell you, just how it felt
When I looked down at my feet and they started to melt.

My nose started running, and so did my hands.
When your legs turn to slush it's not easy to stand.
I'm feeling very sad now, but people say I oughta
Pull myself together, but it's not easy when you're turning to water.

Time's running out, and soon I'll be no more,
Just a heap of old clothes in a pile on the floor
I'm feeling confused, and my life is a muddle.
But it's hard to keep on smiling, when you find you're just a puddle.

I did warn you it was bad, but I got paid what was then a decent sum of money for writing those Christmas songs in the middle of a very hot August afternoon.

*

By the time 2011 came around I was getting tired of all the travelling and moving from hotel to hotel, living out of a suitcase. It was getting to the point where every town and every hotel looked the same. The novelty of a new town or city wears off after a while and once you have spent the day-time visiting the local sights and attractions a couple of times, there is nothing left to do but get up late, sit in the hotel drinking coffee and reading books and magazines while you wait for the time to come to get up on stage again in front of your audience.

Even the occasions when people had kindly given hospitality in their own homes could often become a lonely experience. It had been wonderful while it lasted, but now it was time to take a break. I even grew tired of the performing. Looking back now I can see that at the time I was waking up to a new, deeper sense of spirituality and was finding that singing the same songs night after night, even though it was what the audience wanted and was bringing them happiness, was for me, becoming soul-destroying. Yes, it was time to move on.

Music is still immensely important to me, but the direction has changed. Until recently I have still undertaken the odd gig, maybe two or three a year, singing the songs that have been expected of me, but I feel that even that has come to an end, at least for a while. My spiritual life and my musical life have merged and the songs that I now sing and write reflect that awareness and spirituality. Recent CD recordings have been of mantras and chants, and I now play for, and lead, kirtan sessions in sacred spaces rather than provide background music for drinking and partying. There is a deep joy in leading kirtan, and feeling the energy of call-and-response singing of words that come from the heart. For years I wore the label of musician and entertainer, but that is not who I am. Today, I don't just play the music - I am the music, as are each and every one of us.

Spiritual Life

I don't think that I am aware of any time in my life since early childhood when I have not been conscious of some sort of spirituality. As I have already mentioned, I was born to parents who were members of The Salvation Army, and as such I was brought up in a home where, although I would not describe my parents as being deeply religious, religion did play a large part in my early development. From a very early age I would be taken to Sunday School and would learn the stories from the Bible and become familiar with the life and teachings of Jesus.

Attendance at Sunday School wasn't always welcomed by me especially as it meant having to go twice every Sunday, as well as having to attend the regular adult Salvation Army meetings in both the morning and afternoon as well as the occasional evening meeting that I would be taken along to. Added to this were the two, week-night commitments to band and choir practice. However, this was what I grew up with, a constant exposure to the particular brand of hell-fire and brimstone preaching, together with the constant reminder of the need to repent and be saved.

I remember the first time somebody asked me if I had been saved, I was 7 years old at the time and wasn't quite sure what they meant. Had somebody's quick action stopped me from stepping out into the path of a bus? Had I been in danger of drowning when someone jumped in to rescue me? Had I been dragged to safety from a burning building? It really didn't really make much sense to me at that early age.

Although my church was the Salvation Army, my first school was St Mary's Church of England Primary School on Fuller Street in Kettering. St Mary's was a very "high" Anglican church and every Tuesday morning we would have to walk in pairs, hand in hand, from the school building just a few hundred yards down the road to the church for mass. Most of the mass was in Latin, but we also had to sing the hymns, say the Hail Mary, the Apostle's Creed and the Lord's Prayer. Even now I can still conjure up the smell of the incense and the sound of the bells, which we were told signified the fact that God was present. At school we had regular visits from the priests, Father Sayers and Father Ford, when we would have to learn the catechism and I clearly remember one school term when we had to go to the church after school on one evening a week to walk the Stations of the Cross.

*

An often-heard rebuke when I was growing up was, "*Oh, you're never satisfied, are you?*" whether this was related to the amount of sweets I would want to eat, the lateness of hour that I was allowed to stay up, the number of times I was allowed to play games or just about anything that I enjoyed doing. I suppose I was a bit like Oliver Twist in that I often wanted more, and this certainly applied to my hunger for spirituality.

What I was being taught at the Salvation Army and at St Mary's just seemed to have a big gaping hole in it.

As the years passed and I moved into my teens I felt that there was something lacking in my experience of spirituality and my relationship with whatever it was that we called God. At school we were only taught about the Christian religion, the idea of learning about comparative religions had not yet entered the education system in Northamptonshire. I wasn't satisfied with the teaching I was getting in the Salvation Army, to me it seemed that the rules and regulations took precedence over what the Bible had to say about the teachings of Jesus. I was young, but I couldn't understand why, if Jesus was happy to turn water into wine, Salvationists were forbidden to drink alcohol. If Jesus was happy to be baptized and to commission his disciples to go out and to baptize new believers, why then did the Salvation Army not practice the rite of baptism? I know that these are probably minor things in the big picture of life, but to me as a young teen they seemed to be totally inconsistent with the foundation teachings that Christianity was built upon. Consistency is something that has always stayed important to me.

At the age of 15 I left my secondary school and went on to be a student at the local Technical College. This was a time of great changes and discovery for me, on the one hand my rebellious nature was making itself known in greater ways, it was the time of hippies, the summer of love and flower-power, a time of experimentation and I wanted to be part of it. On the other hand I still felt the grasp of organised religion and the guilt that went along with it. Both of these "pulls" were evident from the two very different groups of friends I had at the college. I became a member of the Christian Union and got to meet people from other denominations and we would discuss the differences in doctrinal beliefs between churches. This led to me joining an ecumenical group in Kettering, called Project One, where we would hold regular discussion evenings and listen to talks from people of varying Christian persuasions. I formed good relationships with new friends from Catholic, Baptist, Methodist, Anglican and Congregational churches, and we would often pay visits to each other's places of worship. I have to say that I enjoyed this alternative to my usual Salvation Army meetings but still there was something missing - where was that powerful presence of God that I felt should be experienced? I would talk with Jehovah's Witnesses and Mormons, and anyone else who might be able to enlighten me, but never managed to find whatever it was that I was looking for.

My other group of friends at that time came about as a result of my interest in music. I wasn't really into the chart music of that time but preferred to listen to what was then described as underground or progressive music. My record collection consisted of bands and artists such as *Tyrannosaurus Rex, The Nice, Principal Edward's Magic Theatre, Nico, Cream, Blodwyn Pig, King Crimson* and *John Mayall.* We all enjoyed listening to the same type of music and would spend time together discussing hippy ideals of love and peace and our shared dissatisfaction at what 1960s establishment had to offer young people. Around this same time, there was much being talked about with regard to mind-expanding drugs, and some people were talking about using these drugs to experience God. Initially, my own experimentation was limited to sitting in a darkened room with a few joss-sticks burning, listening to *Quintessence* on the stereo!

The day came when one of my friends was able to get hold of some cannabis and we all sat around getting stoned and separated from reality, or from the illusion of reality if you prefer to look at it that way. We went on to try other things but the sought-after encounter with the divine managed to elude me, and again, as had so often been pointed out in my life, I just wasn't satisfied.

When I was 17 years old, one of our group somehow managed to accidentally overdose on some pills when we were all together in a local pub. An ambulance was called and he was taken to hospital where his stomach was pumped and a couple of days later he was back with us in the pub, and part of our band of hippy vagabonds. Just a couple of weeks later, one of the girls in the group also overdosed, sadly she didn't recover and she died. She was the same age as me, just 17. I never found out whether it was intentional or accidental, but it was certainly some sort of wake-up call for me.

I wanted my life to have some sort of impact, I wanted it to be worthwhile and, above all, I wanted to realise my spiritual potential. I decided that the only way I could have any chance of making that happen would be to dedicate my life to a spiritual path and just find out where it led me. How would I do it? Well, it seemed to me that the obvious road to take would be one that I was already familiar with.

A few months later, at the turn of the year, I moved away from my parents and from Kettering and went to live in Swansea in South Wales. Swansea was where my family roots were, both my parents having been born there, so it was somewhere safe for me to settle in. I was made welcome by the Salvation Army there, and by its members, and I made the decision that I would train to become a Salvation Army officer which is the Army's version of a minister or vicar.

My training began by attending what were known as "assessment weeks", where a group of high-ranking officers would determine whether I was suitable material for the full-time ministry. Somehow or other, I managed to pass this stage and was accepted for training. After an initial period of studying via a correspondence course, in which I was taught about Biblical doctrine, the history of the Salvation Army, pastoral responsibilities etc., I was sent to be the spiritual leader of a Salvation Army corps (church) in the little village of Resolven in the Neath Valley in South Wales. It wasn't a large congregation, maybe 30 or so, of mixed ages, from young children to those in their 80s. The older people there treated me as a son that they wanted to feed, so meals were never a problem for me, which was just as well, as I found myself living alone in a 3-bedroom terrace house with absolutely no experience of being self-reliant.

On one particular occasion early on in my time at Resolven, I had set out to cook myself some chips for dinner. Never having attempted anything remotely like this before, I was stepping out into what was unchartered territory for me. I knew that the oil had to be hot before putting the chips in, but I didn't know how to tell when it was hot enough. When I saw the smoke and flames starting to creep out of the pan I quickly went into action. Remember here that I am a male, and in the 50s and 60s when I was growing up, boys were not really taught much about domesticity. I did know however, that water is used to put out a fire. I grabbed hold of the chip-pan, took it to the sink and turned the tap on! It would seem that not all fires are put out with water. The resulting explosion of flame totally destroyed the plastic curtains at the kitchen window, at least half of the polystyrene tiles on the ceiling disappeared, while the other half resembled stalactites in an ancient cave. Luckily I escaped with fairly minor burns to my hand - the scars of which are still visible 45 years later when the weather gets really cold.

One of the things that was obvious at Resolven was that if the place was to survive as a place of worship, we needed to attract a lot more younger people so I set about putting on special youth evenings and enlisted the help of a Christian rock-band from a nearby Pentecostal church. These evenings proved to be a great success and it wasn't long before more and more young people were coming along and being converted to the Christian life.

I continued to reach out to people from other denominations for support and to try to learn and understand why they had different beliefs and doctrines. Of particular help to me was the local Baptist minister, Mike Shepherd, and also the folk from the Pentecostal church who provided the band for the youth evenings. Mike and I talked a lot about the sacrament, or rite, of baptism and I decided that if it was good enough for Jesus, it was good enough for me. I was baptised in Sardis Chapel in Resolven whilst still a minister in the Salvation Army; an act that didn't go down very well with my superiors I'm sorry to say, as baptism did not fit in with the Salvation Army doctrine.

I could also see that my Pentecostal friends were experiencing something more through their faith than I was, and I was reaching out to try and discover what it was. There was certainly more life and joy in their religion, more freedom compared to the regimental rules that naturally went with being part of a Christian "Army". I became increasingly disillusioned with where I was spiritually, and finally broke my ties with the Salvation Army. Giving up my role as minister, I moved back to Swansea and, based at The Bible College of Wales, I became a full-time evangelist working mainly with young people on the streets of the city. During this time I attended Mount Pleasant Baptist Church, but never really felt that I belonged there.

Working on the streets I came into contact with a lot of people who were equally disillusioned with the traditional churches. This was the time of the "Jesus People", a movement that grew up in America, which offered an alternative to mainstream Christianity and was more in keeping with the hippy ethos of the time. I had been listening to the music of Larry Norman, a long-haired Christian rock musician, and also to the preaching of one of the leaders of this new movement, the appropriately named Arthur Blessitt, who was travelling around the world in his sandals, carrying a cross over his shoulder, something that I believe he is still doing to this day. I was approached by a group of people who had had some involvement in the "Children of God" sect, but had not been happy with the way that their leader was seen as being all-important and beyond criticism, and they asked me if I would be prepared to take on the responsibility of being their teacher. It was obvious that there were a lot of people who did not feel that they belonged in the established churches and were looking for somewhere that they felt they belonged and would have the opportunity to be part of a dynamic spiritual awakening.

This was also the time of the emergence of the house-churches, where people moved away from the idea that the church had to be centred on a special building and tried to go back to what they believed was the way things were in the early church. Joining together with a small group of friends, my wife Carole and I decided it was time for us to break away from the established denominations and hold open meetings of teaching and worship in our home. We had no idea at the time how many people were feeling the same, but it wasn't long before our numbers grew and we were no longer able to all fit into our house, so had to split into smaller home-based groups, whilst hiring a local hall once a week where all the groups could come together. Students, families and the elderly all came to us and in no time at all we grew from a group of 6 or 7 to over 60 members. From the beginning I took on the pastoral care of the group but we were looked on with a mixture of suspicion and hostility from the churches that many of the people had left in order to join us. It didn't matter to us what people thought, we believed we were moving in the right direction. We shared our lives together, supported one another and witnessed the signs and wonders that were promised in the teachings of Jesus and the apostles.

You might think that I had now found what I was looking for, but this wasn't to be the case. As our community grew, it was felt that we needed to have links with others around the country who possessed more experience in this type of church and the growth we were experiencing. As more people came in, and we looked outside for direction from those who were considered to be modern day apostles and teachers, the feeling that something was not quite right started to nag at me again, but I still didn't know what it was.

As a church community we believed in the power of God, through the Holy Spirit, to be able to heal the sick, and we did indeed see much evidence of people being healed. On the occasions when a person wasn't healed after they had been prayed for and received the laying on of hands, it would usually be put down to that person's own lack of faith. When Donna, my eldest daughter was born, it was discovered that she had a hole in one of the valves in her heart. The natural thing for us to do as a church, and as believing parents, was for us to pray for her healing. We prayed, and nothing happened. We prayed some more and still nothing happened. "*Why not?*" I asked. This couldn't be down to her lack of faith - she was only a baby, with no understanding of what was going on. This was to be the beginning of some deep questioning. I should point out here that Donna went into hospital when she was a little older and able to cope with the operation on her heart, and today she is a perfectly healthy woman. Her healing came about as a result of the skill of the surgeons and hospital staff, rather than through any divine intervention. But that didn't stop me questioning why God might see fit to heal some people and not others, especially when it came to children. The Jesus in the Bible that I had been believing and teaching about said, *"You shall lay hands on the sick, and they shall be healed"*. There was no *"might be healed"* or *"if it is God's will"*. In my mind it was a clearly worded promise that was not being borne out.

I felt that it was only right that, in view of the questioning in my mind, and the doubts that I was having, that I should step down as both a leader and member of the church. How could I stand in front of people and speak with any authority if I had doubts and questions in my own heart and mind? It was time to step back and to ask some questions. Why were the prayers not answered? Why did I believe that they would be? Why, in fact, did I actually believe anything that I believed about God and Christianity? Did I believe it all simply because it was what I had always been taught? Was it just something that had been ingrained in me throughout my childhood and youth that I had just believed without really thinking about it? I couldn't deny that I had had some very real spiritual experiences, and had seen some wonderful things happening in the name of Christianity and God, but what if there was more? What if there was another explanation? What if I had been wrong?

*

After so many years of being involved in the church, I felt that I had a fairly good knowledge of the Bible, so rather than concentrate all my searching there, I decided to look more at the history of Christianity. I wanted to find out how it had developed from its beginnings in Palestine with Jesus and just a hand-full of followers, into the major religion of the Western world. I discovered a fascinating story of a journey that seemed to have more to do with power, manipulation and control of the masses, than it did with spirituality and an individual's realisation of the Divine. The more I read and discovered, the more I wanted to get away from the "religion" and discover the real essence of what we call "God". I wanted to break down the walls that had been built up by men and return to the source, the spirit not the form.

One of the things that struck me as being curious was the need there seemed to have been in the march of Christianity, to bulldoze and clear away anything that came before it. I'm not necessarily talking about the millions of years of world history that was dismissed as never having happened by some branches of the religion, but more about the beliefs and spiritual traditions that had been followed closer to home in Europe and Britain, and were subsequently swept away by the tide of this new religion that was conquering the world. A conquering that, more often than not, took place in a violent and bloody way, rather than one of spiritual awakening or enlightenment.

Christian festivals were established at the same calendar points as the old festivals of the native religion; the celebration of the birth of the Son of God replaced the celebration of the re-birth of the Sun God at the time of the Winter Solstice, the celebration of the death and resurrection was held after the first full moon following the Spring Equinox, a time when the native pagans celebrated the new shoots of Spring breaking through, out of the seeds that had been buried in the earth. However, what seemed to me to be the most significant change was the eradication of the feminine aspect of God. The Divine Feminine had been honoured and acknowledged, not just here in Europe, but throughout the world, however this new religion had only a masculine god, and one that seemed to be full of testosterone and the need to dominate and control. Why had this happened if not to impose power and authority? The strange thing was that I discovered that Judaism, from which Christianity emerged, had traditionally acknowledged the feminine aspect of God and had its own Goddess figures which had since been put aside and neglected. I wanted to discover the Goddess, the feminine part of Divinity.

It made total sense to me, and still does today, that the source of creation should be male and female joined together. That is the way of nature; surely if there is a god or some sort of divine, creative source then it would have the same type of masculine and feminine energies. Even as human beings we all possess feminine traits to our nature; Yin and Yang, positive and negative, Sun and Moon, male and female.

My search for the Goddess took me into modern

Paganism where I found that, in an effort to go back to ancient spiritual roots, a whole variety of groups had emerged that honoured and worshipped the Divine Feminine. Most of these groups made much of our spiritual links to the cycles of nature and the seasons, and the importance of connecting to the natural energies of the earth and the universe in which we live. With the help of some loving and caring people I took particular interest in the teachings and philosophy of Wicca and, over the next few years, received training until I reached what is termed third-degree initiation, which meant that I was regarded as a Wiccan High Priest. Because of my previous involvement in the Christian church, I became known as the "*Wicca Vicar*" and was soon in demand to be interviewed in the press, and on radio and television, about my change of path.

I learnt many positive things through my journey along the pagan path, but I could also see that human ego was being successful in relegating personal spiritual experience to the sidelines. Once again rules and regulations, or in the case of Wicca, laws, seemed to be more important than individual experience. Once a hierarchy is put into place, the individual is stripped of responsibility and no longer needs to trust his or her own instincts and intuition, as somebody else is saying how it should be. Some might say, "*This is the right way to do things*," while others would say, "*no, this is the right way*". I discovered that there were just as many denominations of Paganism as there were of Christianity, with each claiming some sort of ancestral right or divine inspiration that theirs was the authentic path and that others were not genuine. Some claim that in order to be the real thing you must necessarily be initiated by somebody who could trace their line back through generations and could lay claim to being an hereditary witch. Others were quite happy to self-initiate and not be part of a hierarchical system. After much searching and involvement in various groups, it finally began to sink in that spirituality was not something that could be organised, put in a box and labelled. I remembered the words of Jesus, when he said *"The truth shall set you free"*, that was it, spiritual realisation was about liberation and anything that claimed to be spiritual but kept you restricted, imprisoned or in chains, was certainly not *"the truth"*.

I hadn't known it, but I was on a journey to find the truth that would set me free. I had no idea what that truth was, and equally no idea where that truth was to be found, but I would keep searching until I found it. I knew that Jesus was reported as having said *"I am the truth"*, but I felt that the message of the Christian religion was a long way off the mark. I decided to continue to look at the teachings of other religions, but without attaching myself to those religions. I would try to find out if it was even possible to achieve enlightenment, liberation, and fulfilment.

*

As I looked at Hinduism, with its vast pantheon of gods, I was struck by the similarities with both Paganism and, perhaps surprisingly, Catholicism. The many Hindu gods and goddesses, each one relating to a specific quality or aspect of life, seemed to sit well with the multitude of Pagan gods and goddess, each with their own role if you like, in the supernatural realm. In Catholicism it seemed to me that the gods and goddesses had been relegated to the rank of "saint". In keeping with their Hindu and Pagan counterparts, the Catholic saints were seen as having specific responsibilities or qualities. Just as a Hindu devotee or a pagan, might invoke or pray to a particular god or goddess for help with a specific area of their life, so a Catholic would pray to the relevant saint for guidance or for answers.

I found the mythology of Hinduism to be fascinating, with monkey gods, elephant gods, gods of destruction and gods of abundance, gods to remove obstacles - whatever the human needed, there was a god or goddess to meet that need. I was also beginning to see how, in our limited understanding of god, it was possible to create an image of god that would fit in with our needs and help us relate to that energy. I also discovered that in Hinduism, as with every other religion that I looked at, there were divisions and schisms. One Guru would be revered as having all the answers, whilst another Guru with a similar, but slightly different message would also be regarded as a physical incarnation of God. One section would raise the Goddess Kali above all others, whilst another would claim, in an almost evangelical way, that Krishna was the true God above all others. Wherever I looked there were those who were claiming theirs to be the true way.

Maybe I would find that Buddhism had the answer. Once again I found that man had moved away from the teachings that were the foundation of the religion or philosophy, and had built little empires that were at odds with each other. I have had the privilege to meet and share lunch with His Holiness, the Fourteenth Dalai Lama. It was a real honour to experience the energy of this man from whom love and compassion flows so freely and evidently. It came as a shock then to discover a group of Buddhists who so vocally and aggressively speak out against the Dalai Lama, claiming him to be false and a persecutor of their own way of Buddhism. The New Kadampa Movement give special honour to the Deity, Shugden, who is seen by most other Tibetan Buddhists, including the Dalai Lama, as being a negative Deity. The animosity that I witnessed being expressed by the Kadampa monks would appear to be a million miles away from the teachings of the Buddha.

What was becoming clear to me was that all the religions that I was looking at had drifted so far away from the teachings of those that their religion was based upon. I have touched upon this in both my previous books. In *"Be Still"* I wrote a chapter about the differences between religion and spirituality, and in my second book, *"Abiding In The Stillness"*, I wrote the following paragraph, and make no apologies for including it again here.

All the world's leading religions are supposedly based on the teachings of great teachers who themselves spoke out against religion. Jesus, Buddha, Mohammed, Krishna, all spoke about the futility of religion and emphasized the importance of a personal spiritual experience. Jesus said, "The Kingdom of Heaven is within you", The Buddha said

"Peace comes from within you, do not seek it without", An Islamic proverb says, "If you cannot find a temple in your heart, you will not find your heart in a temple", and Krishna, in the Bhagavad Gita says to "abandon all varieties of religion". The Charge of The Goddess in modern paganism also states, "If that which you seek cannot be found within, it will never be found without". There is also a Hindu saying, "What one does not trouble to find within will not be discovered by transporting the body hither and yon".

When I finally came to understand and to realise this, it all made sense. God was not someone or something that was *"out there"*. Just like every other being, I was not, and never had been separated from God. I did not need an intermediary to act as a go-between to put me in contact with God. All the time I had been looking and searching, I had been doing so in the wrong place. The moment of enlightenment had arrived, the cosmic, divine light had never been switched off, simply covered by a shade, and now the shade had been removed and the light was enabling me to see. Enlightenment doesn't mean that you suddenly know everything, but it does mean that the light has broken through and banished the darkness, so that you are able to see and to discover the truth.

The Buddha spent many years searching outside himself for truth, in the end he stopped searching and sat down under a tree. When he stopped looking outside, but turned his attention inwards, he found his enlightenment within. The Prodigal Son in the parable went off in search of happiness and fulfilment, when his searching proved to be fruitless and empty, we are told that he finally *"came to himself"*, which is when he found his way back home to be welcomed by his father.

I spent many years searching for the answer, for the truth, for the way. I read and studied, I sat at the feet of teachers and gurus, I listened to what others said was the way to enlightenment and knowledge, all the time looking to others, looking outside myself. Once again the words of Jesus came to mind, *"Call no man teacher, for you have one teacher who is in heaven"*. He also said, *"The kingdom of heaven is within"*. God, the truth, the way, the light, was not out there, but was within me all the time, as is the case with everyone. It always had been, but I had been looking in the wrong place.

I have a habit of putting my reading glasses down somewhere and then I forget where they are. The only place that I am eventually going to find them is in the same place where I left them. I am never going to find them by looking in places where they are not. Likewise, although we may find hints of it in the lives of other people, we can never find the truth when we look outside ourselves. The truth, God, is within us - inside us. Wherever we are now, that's where God is, there is no need to look any further, just stop what you are doing and look inside.

Whatever it is that we have need of, we can find it within. If we need healing, it is within. If we need guidance, it is within. If we need the answer to a question or a problem, it is within. If we need strength to face a particular situation, it is within. We don't need a church or a temple; we don't need a place built by man in which to find God. We don't need religions made by man where man tells us how to know God. Certainly there are things that we can learn from different religions but I like to view it all as a spiritual buffet. Just as we might go to a buffet to eat the food spread before us, there will be food that pleases the individual's taste buds and there will be other things that are not so pleasing to the taste. When I am at a buffet, I put the things that I want at that time onto my plate, but if there is something that I don't have a taste for I can just leave it where it is, and if somebody else wants to eat it they are perfectly at liberty to do so.

My temple is within my heart, my sacred space is within my heart, my teacher is within my heart, my guru is within my heart, my saviour is within my heart, my God is within my heart. Isn't that just amazing and fantastic, to know that everything that I need is already mine and waiting for me to claim it in my heart? I found, and understood, the reality of the words of Jesus, we really don't need to call anyone teacher or guru, we don't need to put anyone up on a pedestal and bow down to them. Certainly we can learn from others, but just because somebody can teach us a lesson does not mean that they are then to be labelled as some sort of special, divine teacher. My teacher, my guru, my avatar is that divine energy which is inside me, which is God.

The Web of Life

To get from where I started in life, to where I am now, has involved a lot of experiences, a lot of places, a lot of things, and a lot of people.

So many people have been a part of my life, some for just a very brief period in time, some for a lot longer, and even some for an eternity.

I couldn't possibly tell you about all the people whom I consider to have played an important role in contributing to who I am, that would take a lifetime in itself. However, in this section of brief paragraphs, I'm going to talk, in no particular order, about some of those people outside my own family members, who have been instrumental in shaping my life.

The first two people that deserve a mention are both school teachers of mine. One, whom I have already mentioned in an earlier chapter, was **Peter Findlay**, my headmaster at St Mary's school in Kettering when I was 10 and 11 years old, the other being my Maths teacher, who's name I can't remember, at Stamford Road School when I was 13 & 14 years old. Both of them were very different personalities and I include them here for very different reasons. Mr Findlay instilled in me a love for the English language and writing, he encouraged me when I wanted to put together a school magazine and he also entrusted me with the job of being library monitor. A highlight of the school week would always be when he read to us from whatever book the class was focusing on at the time. Unlike any other teachers that I had had, when he read he didn't just read the words, but would give each of the characters different voices and accents, which would make even the dullest of stories more interesting.

Mr Findlay was also a member of Kettering Amateur Operatic Society and would often tell us about the different plays and musicals that he was performing in at the time. He encouraged us to go to the theatre and experience live performances, extolling the virtues of the theatre over television. I remember seeing him once as a pantomime dame, and I was hooked on live theatre from that moment. Eventually in later life, I'm sure as a direct result of his enthusiasm and love for the theatre, I was able to go on to write and direct for the stage, even though I was never able to convince my parents to allow me to go to drama school. Thank you sir.

*

I've tried hard to remember the name of my 3rd year Math's teacher, but without success. He was only at my school for a couple of terms and it was during a time in my life when I was quite rebellious and not really interested in schoolwork. For some reason, this particular teacher was able to look through the veneer and mask that I wore as the class clown and sometime troublemaker. He recognised that I had the ability to excel even though I wanted to keep that hidden and remain as one of the crowd. He took time to talk with me; I mean to really talk *with* me, not at me. He would give up his own time after school to give me extra tuition, as he believed that I was able to work at a different pace to the one being set by the class. For a while I went along to these extra sessions and my work and attitude improved, but the lure of my fellow clowns proved to be too much and he was never able to see any long term result from his efforts to encourage me. I may not remember his name but I do remember that he drove a Zephyr 4 car. The reason I remember that is because we would always make fun of the way he said it with his broad accent, "Zephyr fooer". To this un-named teacher I would like to say thank you for your belief in me and for your time, and to apologise for not appreciating it when it was there.

*

At the age of about 17 I struck up what was probably the most unlikely friendship, with a Roman Catholic nun. In my search for spiritual satisfaction I had joined an ecumenical discussion group and I suppose I should really include all the members of that group as being instrumental in my life's journey, Steve Atterbury and Daphne Hewitt, both of whom were also colleagues of mine when I worked at Kettering Library, Sister Julianne who was a young and attractive nun from either Canada or America (I don't really recall which), Mirren Hyam, and a wonderfully inspiring blind man named David, as well as a handful of other people whose names I can't remember now. One member of the group, who became a life-long friend, right up until she died in 2014, was a Roman Catholic nun with a wonderful West Country accent, **Sister Mary Anita**. Sister Anita and I shared many conversations over the years, and when I left Kettering to live in South Wales she bought me a going-away gift. It was a small book in a bright yellow cover called, *"The Thoughts of Jesus Christ"*. A publication obviously inspired by the very popular *"little red book"*, *"The Thoughts of Chairman Mao"*. Inside the front cover she had written the following words from Psalm 110, *"You are a priest forever after the order of Melchizedek"*, at the time I didn't really grasp the significance of these words, and it was many years later when I had some sort of inkling as to what she was saying. Sister Anita and I kept in regular touch over the following years via letters, which I would always look forward to receiving. Whenever I would return home to see family, we would always meet up, usually for afternoon tea at the convent, where I would be welcomed by the Mother Superior and I would be presented my refreshment on the best china tea-set.

I describe the friendship as unlikely because I was young man with a Salvation Army background, about as far away from Catholicism you could get whilst still being a Christian, and she was a devout nun, thirty years my senior. I am even now so grateful to her for showing an interest in me, with all my questioning and searching, never once putting me down, always showing support and compassion. In later years, Sister Anita became known as **Sister Liz**, as she dedicated her life to working with the sick via the General Hospital in Kettering, where she was known as something of a ministering angel to those who were ill, including several members of my own family. Thank you Sister for always being there and teaching me about accepting, and showing compassion to all people, no matter how different they may be in belief, lifestyle or age.

*

Around the mid 1980s when I was exploring a pagan spiritual path, I would regularly attend and take part in New Age/Psychic festivals. This was a period in my life when I met some wonderfully colourful people, some amazingly eccentric people, some totally weird people and some incredibly inspirational people. One of these influential and inspirational people was the owner of a Pagan shop in Selly Oak in Birmingham, known as Prince Elric's. A respected writer on the subject of Paganism and Western Mystery Traditions, **Rich Westwood** became a great friend at this time and helped me to see beyond the pseudo spirituality of many of the various denominations of modern paganism and also helped me to focus on the roots and the spiritual lessons to be learned by observing the cycles of nature and the seasons. Rich passed away suddenly whilst still at a relatively young age, but I have to believe the timing was right for him, even though it came as a great shock to those he left behind. Thank you Rich for shedding light on the mysteries.

*

Around about the same time, I also got to meet **Paul**

Keown. Paul and his wife Carolyn visited a new age fair in Watford where I had a stand, and we immediately hit it off. At the time Paul was a professional actor, having taken lead roles in various West End productions including Blood Brothers and Jesus Christ Superstar. Carolyn was a professional dancer and dance teacher. The following week, after I met them, I was due to be at the Predictions Fair at the Battersea Arts Centre and Paul invited me to stay with them for the weekend. It was a particularly difficult weekend for me as the divorce from my first wife had just become final. I was happy to not be alone, but to have some company rather than spending the evenings in an anonymous hotel room. Our shared interest in the theatre, together with Paul's interest in the Christian Mystery traditions, ensured that we were able to have some deep and fascinating conversations.

The friendship that Paul and I have shared has lasted over 30 years, and in that time I have witnessed his particular journey and development. He gave up the acting profession in order to train for the priesthood, is now known as Father Paul and is living the life of a parish priest in Wales. For him it has been a journey of challenges and frustrations as he has held firm to his association and belief in Christian Mysticism, and that has been the inspiration that he has shared, probably without even realising it. Thank you Paul for the lesson of staying true to your calling, no matter what obstacles there may be along the way.

*

Not only was **Jim Couza** a big man in a physical sense,

but he was also a man with a big heart and an even bigger reputation. Considered to be one of, if not the leading exponent of the hammered dulcimer, Jim came over to the UK from his home in the United States and established himself on the UK folk-music scene with his virtuoso playing and larger than life performances. His reputation grew as he became in demand from artists such as Peter Gabriel and Björk to work and record with them. Jim & I met whilst I was working with Four Seasons Events, performing at their Mediaeval shows, and I was honoured when he asked me to perform with him and eventually to record a CD with him, which would include some of my own compositions. I had never really rated my own musical ability, I thought I was just about alright, but I thought I knew my limitations. Simply by the fact that this successful and respected musician wanted to collaborate with me and had confidence in what I could do, helped to boost my own confidence. Jim taught me to never undervalue what I could do, that if I felt my talent was limited it was because I had set those limitations. We went on to spend quite a few years working together, playing at venues and festivals around the UK, and he also honoured me on one occasion by asking me to make a guest appearance with his band, The Durbeville Ramblers, on the Avalon Stage at Glastonbury Festival. Jim is no longer with us, but his inspiration lives on. Thank you Jim for instilling in me the confidence to go beyond what I may think are my limits.

*

There are times in everybody's life when somebody

comes along and you receive a strong sense that you already know him or her, even though you have never met them before. Sometimes it feels like there is already a link that goes far beyond this lifetime. **Nikki Coe** was, beyond doubt, one of those people. We met at a craft fair where Nikki was displaying her totally unique ceramic creations; I don't think I had ever seen work quite like it. I introduced myself to her and we instantly became good friends. As we talked together and shared our mutual interest in spirituality, music and creativity it was absolutely clear to us that our connection was a lot older and deeper than could be explained from having just met. I have a total conviction about the idea of re-incarnation, having listened to other peoples' stories and read accounts of experiences, particularly those of children who have been able to recall aspects of previous lifetimes. I have also had my own personal experiences and there have been, and still are, people in my life that I am convinced I have connections that go back much further than this particular incarnation. Nikki was tragically killed when she was still in her early 20s, as a result of a carbon-monoxide poisoning accident whilst putting the finish touches to an exhibition she was working on. There was a leak of fumes from the kiln she was using, which overpowered her, she simply went to sleep and never woke up again. Her husband, Pete, also died tragically at a young age, just a few years later, having been diagnosed with cancer. Nikki taught me about openness, and to always be alert and aware, ready to see and recognise the links that connect us through many lifetimes. Thank you Nikki for turning up again in this life-time, and I expect to see you again in the next, I am sure that once again we will know each other.

There have been many other people in my life that I know have been part of previous incarnations, and sometimes I'm sure that it is possible that somebody who we have known earlier this time around, but has since died, has returned in the form of a new born child and we recognise something in them that reminds us of the one who is no longer physically here. Although I have firm convictions with regard to us having many lives, I don't believe it is healthy to focus too much on those previous existences. Those lives were for then, the life that we have at the moment is for here and now, and our duty is to concentrate on this time around, making the most of it and playing our part in the now, whatever that part may be.

*

Telsa Gwynne was regularly to be found in the audience whenever I was playing my music in Swansea; she loved music and had a couple of particular favourites amongst my songs, and the songs of others that I would perform. We never had much close contact but I would often see Telsa, with her partner Alan, at various events and concerts around the area. We were recently brought back into contact when I bumped into her in town. We talked for a while and she told me that she had recently been diagnosed with cancer. As a result of this meeting she came along to The Centre to receive some reflexology treatment from Kiera. She found the reflexology to be a great help in bringing a state of relaxation and peace. The cancer had now taken hold and was at a stage when nothing more could be done to cure it, and palliative care was the only option.

After one particular stay in hospital she was discharged and sent home for what was expected to be just a couple more weeks of her life. She asked that Kiera would visit her at home, where her husband had arranged for her bed to be put next to a large bay window in the sitting room on the first floor. From where she lay, she was able to look out at the trees in the park opposite. Kiera started making her visits and giving reflexology and other complementary therapy treatments to Telsa and the expected two weeks stretched into another two weeks, and then another and another. I would go along to join Kiera at the end of the treatment and Telsa and I would talk about the gigs where we had met, and about the people and friends that we had in common. Together the three of us would talk about life and about death, and the fact that she was not going to let a little thing like her imminent death stop her from living right up until the end. I looked forward to those times when we sat around the bed with her, the sun coming through the imprint of a pigeon, left when said pigeon decided to fly into the glass window. Amongst the memories we shared was a lot of laughter and a lot of positivity. Towards the end she said that she was getting tired and just wanted to be able to drift off into a deep sleep.

The two weeks that the hospital staff had said she could expect turned into many months, and Telsa finally died peacefully, having never allowed her situation to weigh her down, or to take away her joy of living. Thank you Telsa for the way you handled dying, for your strength and humour, and for not allowing yourself to be sucked into a battle, but rather embracing and actually looking forward to whatever was beyond that last breath.

*

I first came across the music of **Deva Premal & Miten** when I was on tour in Denmark. I had called into a little shop in Helsingør that I had been attracted to by its unusual window display, which seemed to be a very strange mix of things. Alongside crystals and the usual new age paraphernalia of tarot cards, incense, and books on meditation and healing, were religious icons and pictures of the Virgin Mary with the child Jesus. It was strange for me to see these two cultures, which are so often at odds with each other, being displayed side by side.

Once inside the shop I was struck by the calm and peaceful serenity of the place. Alongside one wall was a collection of CDs, many were recordings of relaxation music, music to practise therapies to, music to meditate to, there were spoken word CDs from inspirational speakers offering their teachings and guided meditations, and there were recordings of Tibetan monks and a section of vocal offerings from various people. Whenever I am away from home, particularly in another country, I am drawn like a moth to a flame when I see music that I may not have discovered before. On this occasion I was drawn to a CD called Essence. I had never heard of Deva Premal before, but decided to give it a go. For over 12 years now, that recording has been in the CD Alarm clock at home and every morning we are woken up to the sound of Deva singing the Gayatri Mantra. When we wake up in the morning, our first thoughts affect the rest of our day. If we start the day with negative, complaining, grumpy thoughts we are setting the foundation for a day filled with those thoughts and attitude. If we start the day with gratitude and positive thoughts we are mapping out the future day to be filled with good things. Waking up to, and being aware of the Gayatri Mantra, the words of which have the meaning: "Let us meditate on the divine light, and may our thoughts be inspired by that divine light", helps to lay the foundation for the day ahead. What better thoughts could you possibly have in your head to start the day?

Gayatri Mantra

Om bhur bhuvaha svaha
Tat savitur varenyam
Bhargo devasya dhimahi
Dhiyo yonah prachodayat

Through the music of Deva Premal, I was also introduced to that of her partner, Miten. I could see, in what Miten was doing, the way ahead for my own music. Here was a man, just a couple of years older than me, who had obviously grown up playing the same sort of songs that I had, and yet he had turned his attention to writing and singing songs that came from the heart and the spirit, songs that inspired and energised rather than just entertained. This was a big moment for me and paved the way to me being able to use my own music in a more positive and effectual way. Kiera and I got to meet and spend a little time with both Deva & Miten during their 2015 tour when they played in London. They took time out to help us promote the Peace Mala project of which we are involved. Both Deva and Miten are such beautiful people with beautiful energy. Thank you Deva for helping me to wake up each morning with positive thoughts, and thank you Miten for showing me that I could channel my musical talent into something sacred.

*

Kiera's parents, my mother and father in law, have lived and worked for the past 17 years at Prinknash Abbey, a Benedictine Monastery on the edge of the Cotswolds in England. Initially they were running the visitors' retreat centre and guest-house, but when that closed, Mary took over the management of the shop and cafe, and Robert was looking after the day to day running and upkeep of the estate buildings and grounds. Now that they are both in their 70s, Mary has stepped back from her role at the café and Robert has cut down to working on a part-time basis. During our regular visits to them I have got to know **Father Martin McLaughlin** who, in a community of rapidly aging monks, is one of the youngest and most active.

Fr. Martin and I have had many discussions about religion and faith and I was quite surprised when he had some positive comments to make after reading my previous books. You will know from those books, if you have read them, that my feeling towards organised religion is not exactly favourable and you can't really get a more organised religious institution than a Roman Catholic Monastery. Even more of a surprise to me was when Fr. Martin compared my spiritual philosophy with that of some Catholic theologians and scholars. It had never crossed my mind that there may be priests within the Roman Catholic Church that might actually agree with what I was saying, at least in part, if not the whole thing. He introduced me to the writings of **Fr. Anthony DeMello** and as I read his words I was amazed at some of the things that we shared in common. This in turn has led me to be far more open about reading the works of people that in the past I wouldn't have entertained, because I had already made a judgement based on a belief that we wouldn't see eye-to-eye on any spiritual subject. I still don't see eye to eye with everyone or with everything that I read, but I am able to celebrate the common ground and to learn from the experience and philosophy of others, even when I might not agree with it. Thank you Fr. Martin for helping me to dissolve my prejudices.

*

For as long as I can remember I have wanted to write. In school, my favourite subjects were English Language and Literature. In primary school I started a school magazine, I loved writing stories and using my imagination. I have written songs, plays and musicals. I have written reviews and articles for newspapers and magazines, and I have edited and written for an holistic/spiritual magazine, *Labyrinth*. Up until 5 or 6 years ago the one thing that I hadn't done but really wanted to, was to write a book. I knew it was something that I wanted to do, but I had no idea where to start and, if I did manage to write one, how to go about publishing and distributing it.

I will be forever grateful for the encouragement, information, and lessons given by **Reid Tracy** and **Cheryl Richardson** of Hay House Publishing. Attending a writers' workshop that they facilitated, taught me so much about how to write, what to write and, most importantly, how to publish what I had written. The thought of getting a book published had always been daunting and off-putting; but hearing from Reid and Cheryl how Louise Hay had self-published her first book, *You Can Heal Yourself*, which became a best-seller and led to Louise setting up her own publishing house, showed me that if you are meant to do something there are absolutely no barriers that can stop you. The only barriers are those that we imagine, they are not real. I came away from that weekend workshop, having spoken with both Reid and Cheryl about the book that I believed was inside me, and they encouraged me to go home and do it.

I wrote my first book, set up my own publishing company, *The Centre of The Labyrinth*, and have not looked back since. The process was smooth and simple thanks to Reid and Cheryl helping me to believe that it could be done. I later received the following review from Amy Kiberd at Hay House Publishing:

"I really enjoyed . . . Be Still. It has a lovely, peaceful energy and I think the voice of the author comes across really nicely and definitely makes it easy for the reader

to relate to."

I feel certain that had I not had the opportunity of meeting Reid and Cheryl and receiving their advice and information, I would still be sitting, wondering how I could ever write and publish a book. Thank you for your experience, expertise and encouragement.

*

Michael Eavis, the founder and organiser of the Glastonbury International Festival of Performing Arts, probably has no idea of how much he has influenced and inspired me to get to where I am today. Having been involved in the shadows of the festival since the mid 1980s, it was a massive boost to my confidence and morale when Michael showed his complete trust and confidence in me and asked me to take over as the organiser of one of the four main stage areas of the festival. Thank you Michael for your trust, and for giving me the opportunity to be involved in the organisation of such a marvellous event.

*

I couldn't possibly neglect to mention **Ian "Tich" Thomas** in this section of people who have been instrumental in the journey of my life. Tich and I have worked together for getting on for 30 years now. We have performed together as a duo and in different incarnations of my band, Madra Rua. We have busked on the streets together, played on big stages together, travelled the UK and Scandinavia together, shared hotels, and spent more hours driving up and down

146

motorways in the early hours of the morning together than is healthy for any human being to entertain. Yet we have survived it and still enjoy the occasions when we share the stage. Some days we would drive a round trip of over 500 miles to do a 90-minute gig. Although a fair few years younger than me, I have always regarded Tich as a far better musician and guitarist than I am myself and I have considered it to be an honour that he even considered working with me and my limited number of chords. The great thing about working with Tich is that we seemed to have some sort of telepathic connection when playing music. In all the years we played music together, we never once rehearsed. Often I would throw a new song into the set and he would instinctively know where it was going and how to play it. I very rarely introduced a song but Tich was able to know what it was that I was going to sing, simply from the way I would strike the first chord. Not only has it been an honour to work with him, but it has also been very, very easy. I would not have had such a successful and enjoyable career in music if it had not been for the support and patience of Ian (Tich) Thomas. Thank you Tich, for so many musical memories.

*

In the summer of 2015 I had the privilege of meeting a man whose words and life had already had a huge influence on my own life. Meeting him was a truly life-changing moment and to receive recognition from him is something that is extremely hard to describe. **His Holiness, the 14th Dalai Lama** was a special guest speaker at the Glastonbury Festival in June of that year and, as part of the festival's organisational team, I was invited to join the special lunch that was being laid on for his visit. The fact of having the opportunity of being in the same space as such a deeply spiritual and influential man was, on its own, a humbling and emotional experience.

Before the planned lunch, the Dalai Lama addressed a few thousand festival-goers in the field known as the Sacred Space, where a special platform had been erected for the occasion. I wasn't sure how long he was going to speak for, but I knew that if I stayed to hear the whole talk I would likely get caught in the middle of the crowd as they made their way out of the field, and it would be difficult to get to the place where lunch had been prepared. Thinking practically for a change, I decided to leave before he had finished speaking and make my way to the lunch venue. I arrived there in plenty of time and stood inside the structure, while crowds gathered outside to welcome his arrival there.

When he arrived with his entourage for lunch I was standing in the corner, keeping out of the way, and just feeling privileged to be there. As he came up the steps to go into the dining area, where tables had been set out for about 25 people, he caught sight of me in the shadows as I put my hands together in a "Namaste" greeting. Changing his direction, he came straight towards me and took my hands, still held together, in his, and then placed his forehead against mine, third eye to third eye. He then drew back and indicated with his finger, our third eyes and once again placed his head next to mine and held that position for some time. Almost speechless and very emotional all I could manage to utter was *"thank you, bless you"*. He replied with a smile and returned the blessing. There really are no words to describe how that moment felt.

Once we were all in the dining area, we then had to serve ourselves from a beautiful, but simple, buffet. The humility of the Dalai Lama was striking as he queued with the rest of us to put food on our plates. It was evident that we were in the presence of a man who didn't just talk the talk, but genuinely walked the walk as well.

After lunch was over, I knelt next to the bench where he was sitting, in order to be at eye-level with him and presented him with copies of my books. He took particular interest in the sub-title of *Be Still - Simple Keys to Living a Spiritual Life in a Material World*, saying to me how important it is to remember that we do live in a material world and that there is nothing wrong with that, we must find the balance of spirituality and practicality. As I got up to leave he laughed, took hold of my beard in his hand and pulled my head down to rest on his shoulder. This really was a truly life-changing encounter, that even now I find it difficult to talk or write about without those same emotions rising up in me once more, the same feelings I had on that special day when I received recognition from one of the most spiritually influential men alive today. Thank you for your pure compassion and humility, and for taking time to share your energy with me.

*

The people that I have talked about here are just a handful of the countless numbers who have played a part in my journey, there are many others that I could have mentioned, and I apologise now for not having included them. There are some that, to mention them might cause embarrassment, but nonetheless I honour and respect their influence in my life. There are also many others, whom I have not met but who have also played an important role in my life, through their books and teachings. People like Dr Wayne W Dyer, Ekhart Tolle, Michael Bernard Beckwith, Francis of Assisi, Lao Tsu, Serena Dyer, John Main, Anthony DeMello, Bede Griffiths, Ram Das, Krishna Das and many, many others. To these people I am grateful for the signposts and lessons that they have put before me on this journey.

It is because of all these people, and many more besides, that I am at this present stage of my life. Every single person that has played a part in my history, every single person that I have had some sort of relationship with, whether good or bad, seemingly insignificant or earth-shatteringly momentous, every single person that I have had a conversation with, every single person that has been angry with me, or has caused me to be angry, every single person that has smiled at me, every single person that has brushed past me in life, all of them have been important in leading me to this place. To each and every one of these people, I am grateful and give my thanks. Without you, this moment would be different.

Nothing is Forever

One of the most important lessons that I have learnt in life is that nothing is permanent. I recently witnessed the Tashi Lhunpo Buddhist monks as they very delicately and painstakingly created a beautiful sand-mandala. It is a Buddhist custom to create such a work of art and then to ritually destroy it by sweeping it away, in order to show the impermanence of all things.

People come into our lives and people go out of our lives. No one ever said that just because someone is in your life at a certain time, they would remain in your life forever. We do not own the people in our lives, whether it is our parents, our partners, our children or our friends. We do not have a right to hold on to them and deny them their freedom to be who they really are. This is such an important lesson to learn in both life and death. When it is time for a person in our lives to move on, we must allow it to happen and not try to hold them back.

Throughout my life I have had to say goodbye to many people. Some of them because either I or they moved to a different location, some because we came to a fork on the road we were travelling on and we took different paths, some because for whatever reason we simply lost contact, and some simply because their lives came to an end.

It's not always easy to say goodbye, especially if that goodbye is because of the death of a loved-one. One of the hardest things in life is to let go of someone when they are dying and yet it is so important that we allow them to go. It is totally understandable, but it is basically for selfish reasons that we try to hold on to somebody when their days are ending. We don't want to lose them, we don't want to have to think about our lives without them, and often a dying person will feel that they are being held back from leaving their physical body so that their spirit can journey on to whatever is beyond the threshold of death. It is not uncommon when a family member or members have been sitting with them and willing them to stay alive, for a dying person to wait until a moment when they are left alone, and then to quietly slip away. If we ever find ourselves in that position, when a loved one is coming to the end of their life, the most loving thing that we can do is to give them permission to move on. That permission can make all the difference in allowing them to have a peaceful and good death. I really hope that when it is time for me to leave this earthly body, that those I love will allow me to go peacefully and naturally.

There have been many people involved in my life, some of them have been close friends and played an important part in my journey, others have just been casual acquaintances, but all of them were there at the right time even if we weren't aware of it at that time.

There have been times when their involvement has been really close, even intense at times and then, just as quickly as they came into my life they have gone again, or we have gone in different directions and that is perfectly alright. Nowhere is it written that the same people should be in your life for the duration. Welcome everybody, and allow them the freedom to go again when they choose, knowing that when they do, the purpose of them being there has probably been completed.

The idea that marriage, or a loving partnership, has to be for life, is something that has come from religious teachings rather than from an acceptance of what is often the reality. When we enter into this type of relationship we don't then suddenly own our partner, they don't belong to us, they are not bound to us. I have been fortunate enough, and blessed to have had more than, what some might consider to be, my fair share of loving relationships throughout my life. I have had relationships where I have been hurt, and I have also had relationships where I have been the one who has caused the hurt, but not one of these relationships has been a waste in the big picture of life. It is not a matter of right or wrong, even though at times one of us may have thought that we had made the wrong choice. Everything, every relationship that we go through in our lives, each person's influence has brought us to where we are now.

I have been married three times and have also had other relationships where there has been a measure of love and commitment. One outcome from my first marriage is that I now have two beautiful grown up daughters. There is no way that that marriage could be seen as wrong or a mistake, if that relationship had not happened, then my daughters would not be here now. After seven years together my wife and I split up, at the time it was not a pleasant experience but we have both grown since then and have reached the point where we are now, as individuals. My second marriage ended when we both realised that we probably got on better as friends rather than husband and wife. My wife wasn't happy and I eventually came to the point when I knew that the right thing to do was to let her go, and in a sense to set her free in order for her to live her own life.

I have now been married to Kiera for more than ten of the seventeen years that we have been together. We are blessed in that we both share so many of the same things that give us enjoyment and happiness, and we are both walking on the same spiritual path together. I can't imagine us ever not being together, but I hope that if ever I had to let her go, I would do so with grace and with my blessings. I think though, that at my age, the only reason I would give for her to have to let me go would be when my life is at an end. But who really knows what the future holds.

Those of us who are parents also have to be prepared to let our children go and to free them to live their own lives, and not necessarily the lives that we would want, or choose for them. From my own experience I know how hard it was for me when my parents didn't allow me to follow my dream. I have always tried to not interfere with the direction that my daughters have wanted to take but I confess that it is not always easy.

The natural instinct of a parent is to protect their children and sometimes we can see that they may be heading for trouble, but we do need to allow them to find their own path even if it means that they will trip up sometimes. We can always be on hand to help them up again after a fall, if they want us to do so.

*

Of course, we must never forget that sometimes, the most important teachers who have been in our lives are the ones who hurt us and cause problems in our lives, teaching us through the way that we respond and react. I confess here that I have, more than a few times, taken on that particular role where people have learnt from my negative and unkind actions. As you are reading this you may even recognise that in yourself. There is no need for any feeling of guilt, what has been done has been done, and right now it is what it is.

No doubt I have hurt people through my words and deeds, and there have been times when I have been untruthful in both actions and words. Even in writing this book you could say that I have not been entirely truthful as there is so much that I have omitted to say. It probably wouldn't be helpful to anyone were I to write about every experience in my life that has brought me to where I am now, and I dare say that some would be needlessly hurt had I done so. There have been occasions when I have not acted when I should have acted, and times when I have acted and spoken when it would have been better to have kept my peace. Whatever has happened in any of our lives has all been part of the weaving together of the life that we now live, and if we have hurt others and done wrong, we can take the opportunity to say sorry if it is right to do so, but we also have to be conscious of not opening up old wounds and causing even more hurt. Sometimes we just have to forgive those who hurt us and also to forgive ourselves, and keep moving along the road before us.

Let me just say it again, nothing that ever happens in life is without purpose. We learn from every experience, every word spoken, every decision taken, even if at the time those experiences might not be pleasant, or those words hurtful and destructive, or the decision taken appeared to be the wrong one. Everything in the past has resulted in the now. Without the past, we would not be where we are in this moment.

I don't for one minute have a belief in a god who sends suffering and pain to us in order to teach us important life-lessons. As a loving, caring father there is absolutely no way that I would cause my children suffering so that they could learn a lesson. Which one of us as parents has ever said, "Here, let me pour boiling water over you to teach you that it will burn you"? Or which one of us has ever pushed their child into a stream of fast-moving traffic in order to teach them to look both ways before crossing the road? If you believe that your god would cause pain, hurt and suffering to teach lessons, then I would suggest that you remove any idea of him/her/it from your consciousness. God does not cause hurt and suffering, we cause our own pain by the way we act and re-act to situations and people.

You may ask, *"what about such things as sickness and terminal illness?"* God doesn't ever send such things to us, they are simply things that may happen along the way and the way we respond to them makes all the difference to whether we allow them to control or kill us, or whether we continue to live our lives with joy and purpose in the face of problems and difficulties that we may face. It is our responses to events and difficulties that have brought us to where we are, not the events themselves.

Someone once said that *"life is a sexually transmitted, terminal condition"*, there will, without doubt, come a time when we all must draw our last breath and face death. For some of us it will be through illness or health problems, others will die quietly and peacefully in their sleep, yet others may be killed in an accident or by an act of violence. Death is something that none of us can avoid, but let me repeat, God does not cause us to suffer in any way, but the Divine energy inside us enables us to learn from our suffering and to deal with the consequences of our suffering.

On the road of our lives we will likely come up against many obstacles, but the Ganesh in our hearts helps us to overcome those obstacles. There will be brick walls and barriers but the Kali in our hearts enables us to destroy the things that would block our path. There will be people who irritate, hurt and upset us along the way but we can allow the Christ in our hearts to fill us with love for those people.

When we have travelled our journey and we finally

reach the moment of our physical departure from this life, may we be able to look back and realise that truly all things have been working together for our good and come to a realisation that *"The End is Insight"*

Afterword

This has been a brief account of the life, up until this moment, of the one given the birth label, John Reeves and who later became known as Jim Fox. It is a story of things that have happened to me and things that I have done, a story of many changes - changes of career, changes of home, changes of direction and changes of awareness. Somewhere, right from the beginning, has been who I really am. Not always visible, not always recognised, but always there. I am not the things that have happened to me. I have been knocked down but I am not knocked down. I have been raised up, but I am not raised up. I have been hurt, but I am not hurt. Neither am I the things that I have done in the past or the things that I do now. I have often had to run for the bus, but I am not a runner. I am also not what I have - I have a mobile phone, I am not a mobile phone. I have a body, I am not the body, I am the soul.

I am, as are all of us, the divine essence that is the source of all things.

I am.

I am a light
A light in the world
A light in the darkness
A light of hope
A light of truth
A light of peace
A light in the world
I am a light.

The Centre

Kiera & I had long shared a vision of setting up an Holistic Centre, providing a space for complementary and holistic therapists to offer their treatments in a professional and peaceful environment. One of our aims right from the beginning was to be able to offer some of our treatments to those who were living with cancer and other life-limiting illnesses, and also to their carers. We wanted to be able to offer these treatments, either free of charge or in exchange for a donation.

Through Kiera's work as a palliative care nurse and also as an End Of Life Companion and Soul Midwife, together with my own personal experience of caring for family members with cancer, we are very aware of the benefits of holistic therapies for both the patient and the carer. We don't claim to offer a cure through our therapies or a substitute for conventional medicine, but we do believe that holistic therapies can certainly help and support those who are having to deal with their illness.

Recognising that healing is not just about dealing with symptoms, but should be approached holistically - addressing the whole person, The Centre also provides a sanctuary for meditation and a training space for workshops and classes.

As well as the comfortable therapy rooms, The Centre also has a beautiful "Peace Garden", where visitors can just sit or make use of the summer house to experience some stillness in the heart of the city.

If you would like to help support the work of The Centre, visit the website at **www.thecentre-swansea.co.uk** where you can make an online donation.

The Elephant In The Room

A conversation a few years ago with artist and creator of the *"A Graceful Death"* Exhibition, Antonia Rolls, led to the planting of a seed. The seed was watered and fed, looked after and the seedbed was weeded, until at last it grew and bore fruit. An abundance of fruit that refreshed, sustained and strengthened all who tasted of it.

When we first talked about organising an event to raise awareness around the subject of death and dying, we had no real idea how we were going to bring everything together, or how successful it would be. We knew that we wanted Antonia to bring her wonderful exhibition of End of Life art to Swansea, and we also knew that we wanted Doctor Penny Sartori to be involved and to share her research into Near Death Experiences. A couple of years ago Kiera and I had seen a production of Laura Wade's play, *"Colder Than Here"*, and I knew then that one day I wanted to direct my own production of it. It wasn't going to be enough for me to put on a small event, if it was going to be done, it had to be something worth doing.

The first thing to do was to find a venue, somewhere big enough to host the talks and workshops we wanted to include, space for the *"A Graceful Death"* exhibition and other exhibition stands, and a stage and auditorium where we could present the play and also a musical concert. Having found the venue, we set about approaching various speakers and workshop facilitators to invite them to be part of, what we were now calling, *"The Elephant In The Room"* - that thing that we are all aware of, but nobody wants to talk about. The response was varied, and sometimes unexpected. Many of those that we thought would be interested, politely ignored us, whilst others nearly bit our hands off in their eagerness to be part of this event. After several months we were finding that we needed to extend our programme of talks in order to fit everyone in who wanted to speak.

We then set about holding auditions for the four cast members of our play and we were inundated by a grand total of four who wanted to audition! It turned out that the four were all perfect for the individual parts they were auditioning for - we didn't have to make a choice, as the right people turned up for the roles and so we began the task of rehearsing.

We had no problem in putting together a line up for the opening concert and, even though we had agreed to pay expenses to those taking part, every one of them said that they would do it for free, as any money raised over the four days was going towards the work of The Centre in providing support and free complementary therapy treatments to those living with cancer or other life-limiting conditions, and also to support Antonia's A Graceful Death project.

Posters and flyers were designed, printed and distributed, press-releases were sent out, articles were written, the media was contacted, cakes were baked and we slept very little. Time moved on and finally everything was in place for us to open the doors on The Elephant In The Room. All we needed now was for people to come through those doors.

And come, they did. Over the four days of the event people came and listened to the talks, viewed the art-work, were entertained by the music, laughed and cried at the play, talked about their own personal experiences of bereavement, of facing up to the prospect of losing loved-ones, and embracing their own mortality. Together we supported each other, cried with each other, laughed with each other and ate mountains of cake.

When we first started out on this journey with the Elephant, we had no idea how we would fund it - we had no money, only a vision. The whole event cost us over £2,000 to stage, but we wanted it to be accessible so, apart from the concert and the play, we wanted to make sure that entrance to the talks and exhibition would be free. We knew that there would be no point in worrying about the money - so we didn't. If we didn't cover our costs, there was always the credit card to fall back on. We didn't want to use plastic, but we weren't going to be put off doing what we felt was something we had to do and that we had a real passion for.

When the final visitor left on the Sunday evening, and all the paintings and stands had been packed away, and the last of the volunteers and exhibitors had gone, we knew that we were nowhere near covering our costs, but that didn't matter, we had done what we had set out to do and, as far as we were concerned, it was a resounding success. It looked like we were going to need that little plastic card after all, but what the heck, it had all been worth it.

In my previous books and talks I have always said that The Law of Attraction is not about just asking for what you want and it will come to you, just because you believe and put out positive energy. The Law of Attraction is about being in that place of Stillness, where you realise your connection with the divine source, whether you call that source god, spirit, universe, divine mind or whatever name you want to give it. When you are in that place or realisation, you will know what path you should be taking. You will know what it is that you should be doing with your life. You will know your own personal dharma. It is then that whatever you need to accomplish your purpose and to reach your goal, will be attracted to you.

When Kiera and I got home that Sunday night, we found that somebody had left an envelope for us. Inside the envelope was a cheque for nearly £800. That cheque, added to all the other donations from the last four days, meant that the little piece of plastic could stay in the drawer and everything that needed to be paid, could be paid. Thank you.

That is the Law of Attraction at work and in evidence.

We are eternally grateful to all those who supported, whether it was with time or money or simply encouraging words. We are grateful to the divine source of all things for leading us towards The Elephant In The Room so that we could encourage people, not to ignore it but to talk about it.

Our aim, through The Elephant In The Room, is to help to break through the mystery, fear and confusion and to take away the stress and worry that is so often faced at the end of life, whether it is our own or that of a loved one. By covering such topics as End-of-Life care, Funeral Planning, Advance Decisions, Wills, Organ Donation etc, we hope to encourage people to talk openly with their families and friends and to acknowledge that thing that we have a tendency to ignore.

After the success of our first event, we felt that it would be right to take The Elephant on the road and visit other towns and cities, and we have since put on events in Dorset and West Wales with plans for future events in different parts of the country. We have a real passion for this work and believe that doors will open, and the support will be there to enable us to reach as many people as are ready.

If you would like to know more about The Elephant In The Room and/or how you can be involved in bringing it to your town or city, please get in touch via elephantintheroominfo@gmail.com
or visit
www.theelephantintheroom.btck.co.uk

Acknowledgments

I want to offer my grateful thanks to all those who have inspired and encouraged me in the writing of this book, and to all who have supported me in my work.

Particular thanks must go to Kiera Jones for her patience in going through the manuscript, making suggestions for changes, and remedying grammatical errors.

A big thank you to Richard Kingston of Young Rascal for the front cover picture. www.youngrascal.co.uk

About the author

Jim Fox is an inspirational writer and speaker, based in South Wales. After spending many years as a professional musician, performing throughout the UK and Scandinavia, he trained as a Sound Therapist and, together with his wife, he runs an Holistic Centre providing various therapies, training & workshop facilities, including offering free support and therapies to those living with cancer and life-limiting conditions, and their carers.

The End is Insight is Jim's third book; he also has recorded a number of CDs of spiritual mantras and leads regular Kirtan sessions.

For more information about Jim's work, his recordings and writings, please visit

www.jimfox.info

Also Available
By
Jim Fox

Be Still
Simple Keys to Living
A Spiritual Life
In a Material World

Published by
The Centre of The Labyrinth
ISBN 978-0-9573855-0-4

Abiding In The Stillness
Realising a
Life of Abundance

Published by
The Centre of The Labyrinth
ISBN 978-0-9573855-2-8

Available from
www.jimfox.info
Kindle Editions available worldwide from Amazon

Life Celebrations

More and more people want to celebrate milestones in their lives, whether it be Weddings/Handfastings, Naming Ceremonies, or Funerals, without the religious dogma and ritual that is so often associated with them. Jim Fox & Kiera L Jones are available to officiate at all life-celebrations and are happy to provide the ceremony that you require, taking into account all that you want, which may not necessarily be what others expect of you. Whether you want an element of spirituality or would prefer a simple humanistic ceremony, Jim and Kiera will work with you, combining their experience and your preferences to make the occasion special and memorable.

For further information, or to discuss your requirements, you can contact them at: info@jimfox.info

#0132 - 111217 - C0 - 210/148/10 - PB - DID2060002